Crystal Hansen g̲         ̲  ̲  ̲        who are trying
to improve their p̲  ̲  ̲  ̲  ̲  ̲ ̲motional health, and to lose weight
and keep it off!

Howard Flaks, MD, Beverly Hills bariatric physician

*Skinny Life* takes all the guesswork out of weight loss. Crystal makes
it fun, exciting, and effortless. I love her work!

Tony O'Donnell, PhD

Crystal's book is helpful for everyone—not just for people wanting
to be skinny! Her commonsense, practical, faith-based approach
inspires us to create respect for our body, the incredible gift our
spirit inhabits. By changing our thought patterns, we can build a
happy, healthy life.

Olivia Newton-John

Finally a fresh new perspective on being the best (nonfat) you. No
fad diet here, instead a practical mental reset for a healthy life. If
you are overweight or thinking about being overweight this book
will change your mind. It will change you and your relationship
with food forever!

"Amazon John" Easterling, founder, Amazon Herb

I discovered long ago when I was a young man picking natural tea leaves in the Colorado Mountains, that healing, wellness, and fitness are only achieved when your approach is holistically integrated. *Skinny Life* is a breakthrough book that captures the truth of that wellness journey and delivers it honestly. If you want a breakthrough in your health and fitness, you *will* find many secrets inside this wonderful book!

Mo Siegel, Founder, Celestial Seasonings Tea

*Skinny Life* is chock-full of wisdom and intelligent answers to the problems that plague people relentlessly with their health and fitness. Crystal Dwyer Hansen, thank you for pulling this book together so that people can finally get the truth on how to integrate the mind, eating, and movement. The people I am coaching will benefit greatly from reading and living the sage guidance inside these pages!

Dr. Mick Hall, Developer of "35 for Life"

C-1

# skinny life®

the secret
to physical,
emotional, and
spiritual fitness

# Crystal Dwyer Hansen

WORTHY®
PUBLISHING

Copyright © 2015 by Crystal Dwyer Hansen

Published by Worthy Books, an imprint of Worthy Publishing Group, a division of Worthy Media, Inc., One Franklin Park, 6100 Tower Circle, Suite 210, Franklin, TN 37067.

WORTHY is a registered trademark of Worthy Media, Inc.

HELPING PEOPLE EXPERIENCE THE HEART OF GOD

eBook available wherever digital books are sold.

Library of Congress Cataloging-in-Publication Data

Hansen, Crystal Dwyer.
Skinny life : the secret to being physically, emotionally, and spiritually fit / by Crystal Dwyer Hansen.
pages cm
ISBN 978-1-61795-493-1 (paperback)
1. Weight loss--Popular works. 2. Weight loss--Psychological aspects--Popular works. 3. Weight loss--Religious aspects. I. Title.
RM222.2.H2284 2015
613.2'5--dc23

2015002761

Many of the names and identifying characteristics of the individuals in this book have been changed to protect their privacy. Some of the individuals described are composites of two or more people.

Because each individual is different and has particular dietary needs or restrictions, the dieting and nutritional information provided in this book does not constitute professional advice and is not a substitute for expert medical advice. Individuals should always check with a doctor before undertaking a dieting, weight loss, or exercise regimen and should continue only under a doctor's supervision. While we provide the advice and information in this book in the hopes of helping individuals lose weight, multiple factors influence a person's weight, and individual results may vary. When a doctor's advice to a particular individual conflicts with advice provided in this book, that individual should always follow the doctor's advice.

Published in association with Ted Squires Agency, tedsquires.com

For foreign and subsidiary rights, contact rights@worthypublishing.com

ISBN 978-1-61795-493-1

Cover Design: Christopher Tobias, tobiasdesign.com
Cover Image: Michael Munson
Interior Design and Typesetting: Bart Dawson

*Printed in the United States of America*
15 16 17 18 19 RRD 8 7 6 5 4 3 2 1

*They say one spark can create a flame*

*that can create a wildfire.*

*Mom, you are that spark.*

*This book is dedicated to you for helping*

*to cause a beautiful wildfire of*

*truth in health and fitness.*

*Let it continue to spread for the good of all.*

# Contents

# Foreword

Look around you anywhere in our modern society, and you'll see the problem and a noticeably ineffective set of solutions surrounding weight and obesity.

This book is rich with clear solutions and tools that cut through the confusion, noise, and empty promises of most diets and weight-loss programs.

In my practice involving the brain and brain-imaging studies for many years, I've observed the powerful driving force of the mind and how it controls our emotional states and physical bodies. When you learn through Crystal's insights and techniques how to purge a destructive mind-set and then integrate a constructive mind-set, you can cause a complete shift in your health and fitness.

I've seen firsthand how those mind-set changes can transform everything about a person, including their physical and emotional states.

The book is thoughtful and comprehensive so that you can finally see how to get all of the pieces of the weight puzzle—your mind-set, your eating habits, and healthy daily movement—to fall easily into place.

*Skinny Life* takes you on a smart, easy journey through the truth about the inescapable connection of your mind, body, and spirit and how to bring them together to triumph over weight issues and their mental and emotional entanglements.

When you read this book, Crystal's life experiences and authentic, comfortable style make you feel like you're rocking on a porch on a summer day, sipping lemonade sweetened with stevia (please hold the sugar to keep your brain healthy). You can't help but enjoy it!

—Daniel G. Amen, MD
Founder, Amen Clinics
Author of *Change Your Brain, Change Your Life*
Coauthor of *The Daniel Plan*

# Introduction

Something is wrong with the way we've been trying to lose weight in America. Have you noticed? We spend billions of dollars on weight loss in the United States each year, but people are carrying more excess weight than ever! What is going on?

Here's the scoop: you can never permanently fix a problem if you address only the symptoms and not the cause. That's where *Skinny Life* comes in. This book is unlike any you've ever read about weight issues.

Since you picked up a book with this title, you have probably experienced an issue with weight at some point in your life, perhaps even for most of your life. Starting today, let's seriously consider your weight issue, because, as you know, excess weight can be a huge risk factor for disease as well as destroying your confidence and sense of well-being.

Let me ask you a few questions to help you see how this book will be different than all the other weight-loss books or programs you may have tried.

- What if you discovered that all of your weight issues are in your mind?
- What if you could uncover all the ways you are subconsciously sabotaging your weight-loss efforts?
- What if you could change your diet *not* as punishment for being overweight, but as a rewarding act of self-love, self-respect, and self-honor?
- What if you could throw away your scale and resolve your weight issues permanently?
- What if you found out that you are *not* destined to be overweight?
- What if you realized you are a masterpiece in the making?
- What if you could learn how to use your mind to eat and exercise so that your lifestyle is changed for the better?
- What if you became an expert on quality foods, effective exercise, and supplements?
- What if you decided to change your life once and for all—and actually had a practical, easy, doable way to stick with it?

Imagine knowing exactly what foods to shop for to make the healthiest, most delicious, nutrition-packed meals you have ever eaten. Imagine knowing what eating choices to make every time, no matter where you are or what you are doing. Imagine discovering new and easy ways to burn hundreds of calories and rev up your metabolism, even if you have only five or ten minutes to exercise. Imagine enjoying healthy activities, having a blast doing them, and looking forward to the next session! Imagine that you are living the healthiest, most youthful, fit life possible—and doing it easily and naturally.

*Skinny Life* will show you how.

## Get to the Root

Most programs tell you to eat less and exercise more. Is there anyone who doesn't know that already? So why do we self-sabotage and do the opposite of what we know is good for us? Why do we start yet another weight-loss regimen and then quit again on ourselves?

No matter how much you know about exercise and eating right, that knowledge is not going to make a difference until you can control the behaviors and habits that *drive* you to overeat and cause you to neglect your need for healthy movement and nutrition.

*Skinny Life* brings you the real "skinny" on fit, slim, and healthy. I have designed this book to help you get to the source of the problem, which is always in the mind. I'll help you root out your weight issues where they *start* so they don't continue to trip you up. And here's a big difference: your Skinny Life journey will start from a place some of us seem to have forgotten—self-respect, self-love, and self-honor.

In my years of practice as a life coach, I've worked with people to resolve all kinds of issues, including depression, phobias, lack of self-confidence, performance anxiety, starting over, and weight control. The weight issues began to really tug at me because I knew what people were doing wasn't working. The way we have historically dealt with weight issues in America will never work. We must treat the entire person, not just his or her appetite.

It's easy to be skeptical when you've been through other

weight-loss programs; when you've tried to stick to diet or exercise regimens but somehow they just haven't worked out. The Skinny Life program speaks to you in a different way from any other weight-loss program on the planet—I'll speak to you as a whole person. This program isn't about counting calories and weighing yourself; it is about understanding yourself, loving yourself, and learning to support yourself and your habits all the way to Skinny Life freedom.

Whether you're a busy executive, a chronic emotional eater, or a new mom feeling overwhelmed, *Skinny Life* is designed to help you shift the belief patterns that have kept you stuck in a negative image. I'll show you how to create a brand-new relationship with yourself and with food so you start making healthy food choices. I'll also help you integrate simple habits so you will easily weave fat-busting, metabolism-revving movement into each day, and keep it fun and interesting.

## My Own Epiphany

I created *Skinny Life* out of my own rebellion. One day, years ago, I felt the need to weigh myself, triggered by thoughts of what I had eaten in the last twenty-four hours. It was a familiar urge prompted by the voice in my head that was forever reminding me, *Don't let down your guard about your weight or it could sneak up on you.* So many men and women experience a similar voice when they are feeling disconnected and out of control with their eating habits and weight. My unhealthy relationship with food didn't necessarily show up as my being terribly overweight, but it was the same unhealthy cycle nonetheless.

In my stress from running a business and as a mother of three kids with lots of commitments and projects, I would disconnect from my health and eat all kinds of junk and then punish myself afterward with big-time deprivation. That day, as I headed into my bathroom to the scale, I suddenly realized how absurd the whole cycle was. I decided I would not spend another day beating myself up about what I ate, how much I weighed, and whether I could hold it all together. I said out loud, "I'm never going to weigh myself or worry about what I eat again. I'm going to learn exactly what I need to do and eat to be healthier and more fit than I ever have been. I believe it will then be natural for me to be slim and I won't have to obsess about it anymore."

And you know what? It all came true. Everything *did* change for me from that moment on. Why? I began looking at food not as an enemy, but as an important part of my health-support system. Instead of staring at glazed doughnuts and asking, *Should I or shouldn't I?* I approached eating decisions like an artist picking the most fabulous shade of paint for her painting, asking instead, *Is this going to give me the vital energy I need, the beauty I want, and the health I deserve?*

As a result, instead of being drawn to eating things that were unhealthy and low in nutrition, things that would rob me of my best self, I naturally started seeking healthier foods. I was no longer the old me who had to exercise intense willpower and strength to not eat the caramel muffin—and then felt like a failure when I did and punished myself with a commensurate amount of deprivation. I saw the bad habits I had fallen into and realized it just didn't feel good inside to be in this destructive loop.

It was like making a decision that I would wear only the finest, highest-quality clothing so I would always look my best. I started having so much fun making positive decisions about my health, and soon it became normal to me to seek out the best-quality, most nutritious, slimming foods available. I found that I loved eating even more from my new paradigm. I was creating a healthy relationship with my body and with food.

The path to that freedom is available here and now for you. I spent several years carefully creating the Skinny Life program so that anyone could immerse herself in the tools and resources that will speak to her subconscious and conscious mind and allow her to make this shift in the most accelerated way possible. In each chapter you'll find Skinny Life Bottom Lines—essential truths for life change—as well as Skinny Life Toolboxes—exercises you can do to put what you are reading into practice.

My purpose and dream in writing this book and creating the Skinny Life program is that you, too, will be empowered to let go of that punishing model in your mind and begin to accept and love yourself all the way to Skinny Life abundance.

Successful mastery of weight, health, and fitness can be thought of as a triangle. The components of the Skinny Life success triangle are Mind-Eat-Move, with Mind being the top point and Eat and Move the bottom points. We'll spend the first part of this reading journey focusing on the mind aspect, because ultimately every behavior or habit you have now or ever will have is controlled by your thought patterns. Most programs don't work for the long term because they start at the wrong place. We'll take a deep dive into your perceptions, thoughts, and awareness. Our goal will be to create a new, healthy self-image and new belief patterns that support your greatest health, fitness, and well-being.

## Where It Starts

When I discovered the Skinny Life for myself and then began teaching it to my clients, I found there was one essential step I had to take before anything else could happen. This is the one thing we all have to experience before we can taste (pun intended) the success and freedom we desire with our health and fitness. That one thing is *commitment*.

When you get to a point in your life when you recognize the status quo is no longer acceptable and you yearn for something much better, you have to begin with a commitment to yourself. Otherwise you are essentially leaving doors of failure wide open. When you make a commitment, you take responsibility and put yourself in the driver's seat of your life. You're declaring that you recognize that you are empowered by God and that when you make a decision on behalf of yourself, that decision is powerful.

Are you ready to make that commitment? If so, I want you to take a really deep breath and just hold it for a moment before you exhale. Good! Here we go!

As you read this book, be prepared for a journey of realization, recognition, and resolve. This is some of the most important work you'll ever do, because your body is where you will reside all your years on this earth. As you begin to understand what you are in your body, why you exist, and the power gifted to you by God, you'll become infinitely masterful at creating a better version of you than you ever thought possible. The fittest, slimmest, healthiest you is connected to this amazing gift from God . . . your body.

Do this for yourself. Let's take the Skinny Life journey together. In the pages that follow, I will help you to become your healthy, young-looking, lean, fit best. And you are going to love it!

## Affirmations

The things you tell yourself matter. I believe in the power of positive affirmations. Affirmations are a simple but important tool in transforming yourself as you ignite positive feelings inside and rekindle them every day. Each chapter of this book will conclude with several affirmations to encourage you in your Skinny Life journey.

I recommend you record these affirmations in the notes on your smartphone or tablet and on sticky notes you can put in strategic places. Repeat these affirmations to yourself throughout the day. Repetition helps us change old thought and behavior patterns.

Do not be surprised if you feel emotional or even begin to weep when you start this process. Our bodies store a lot of negative energy, and not just in our minds. As you begin to release this stored negativity and even some of the emotional pain tied to it, it's highly possible that you will feel a sense of release and even relief washing over you. That is healthy. Embrace it and don't feel embarrassed about it. This is exactly what you need.

Eventually these affirmations will become your beliefs because the truth will begin to resonate inside you. These new beliefs will begin to form your new identity. These will become the seeds that will grow new default patterns, habits, and actions that support your best fit, slim you—a new, Skinny Life version of you that is emotionally healthy and free!

# Affirmations

I am ready now to make this
self-caring commitment to myself.

It is time for me to make this
self-caring commitment to myself.

Everyone will be fine as I make this
self-caring commitment to myself.

No one else is responsible for me.
I am responsible for myself.

The Skinny Life is my path to freedom from weight issues.
I am ready to be free.

I am ready to be connected to my
greatest health and fitness.

# Part One

# The Truth about
# Weight Issues

# It's about a Relationship

Have you ever been dissatisfied with something in your life and said, "I just want to know how to fix this! I'm ready to change. I'm ready to be better. Just show me the way. God, you know the truth, and I'm ready to hear it. Sorry if I haven't been listening. Um . . . I'm waiting . . ."

That's the place Coralynn was when I met her.

Coralynn responded to an ad I ran for a test group for my new weight-loss program. She came into my office for her first appointment, and I couldn't help but notice her pretty face and a bright spirit. When I started doing her information intake, it was clear that in spite of her beaming presence she had fought a form of darkness for a very long time. Like many other clients I'd worked with, Coralynn's emotional battle took place in the realm of eating, food, and a negative body image. The very thing that God made necessary for our human survival each day—food—had become, in Coralynn's world, an evil that threatened to destroy her happiness.

In fact, Coralynn felt that both food and even her own body were her worst enemies. She had been on diet after diet and at different times had punished herself through excruciating exercise routines, only to fall off those strict regimens and end back at the same place: hating herself for failing, hating her body, and being afraid of food and how it controlled her.

Not every experience of dieting and weight loss is as extreme as Coralynn's, but the truth is that weight issues are disturbingly pervasive in the United States. Our inability to connect to, understand, and manage our bodies and weight can lead to devastating consequences in our own health and sense of well-being, not to mention staggering costs in our country's health care.

Here are the sobering facts:

- We spend almost $60 billion per year on diets and weight-loss products[1], yet people are heavier than ever before in history.
- Up to two-thirds of dieters who lose weight will regain more weight than they lost on their diets.[2]
- More than 35 percent of Americans are obese, and almost 70 percent are overweight.[3]
- America has triple the number of overweight kids and teens now than in 1963.[4]
- Childhood obesity is the number-one health concern among parents in the United States, topping drug abuse and smoking.[5]
- For the first time in history, we could be looking at a generation of kids whose life expectancies are shorter than those

of their parents. In 2012, more than one-third of children and adolescents were overweight or obese and nearly 18 million children under the age of five are estimated to be overweight.[6]

Do you see what I'm seeing? Something is wrong here, folks! What we're doing isn't working. In fact, researchers at Vanderbilt University said, "In the United States the failure rates of diets are 90–95 percent. This outstanding rate of failure proves the point that the diet programs have not been designed to address the correct set of problems."[7]

In a society where we have more resources and information than ever before, we are completely out of control! We don't understand yet what we need and don't need. We're out of touch with ourselves. We're disconnected from perhaps the most important earthly gift God gave to us: our bodies.

## Get the Real "Skinny"

In the Skinny Life program my goal is to empower people of all sizes and shapes to get the real "skinny," or the bottom-line truth, on what it takes to be truly and holistically healthy, fit, and balanced in their minds and bodies. Instead of trying to meet society's impossible standards of beauty, especially for women, Skinny Life focuses on finding the healthiest version of you by celebrating the gift of your body and creating awareness about all you can do to honor and care for it. The Skinny Life is meant to be a journey of peace and serenity. The goal is to understand your body and how it relates to your life in a more integrated way. If we continue to live detached from our bodies, metaphorically speaking, we can't expect to have the levels of success and happiness God meant for us to have.

 **Skinny Life Bottom Line:** The goal is to understand your body and how it relates to your life in a more integrated way.

Beauty does come in all sizes. But for every size and shape, it's important to feed and care for yourself with all that is good, recognizing and avoiding what's not good, so you can truly walk this earth doing and being all your Creator meant for you to do and be.

## Live and Let Live?

Popular books today urge you to embrace your overweight condition, claiming that your physical body doesn't matter and it is what's inside that counts—a sort of just-celebrate-your-size-and-keep-moving approach. I beg to differ. While true beauty and happiness do radiate from the inside out, if you're not honoring your body and you choose to remain disconnected from the way you're treating yourself at the physical level, then it's like allowing a big, dark cloud to invade your well-being. You see, all parts of you are interconnected. One part of you cannot be adversely affected without adversely affecting the other parts of the whole you.

Think about a time when you felt great about your health and fitness. Your sense of serenity probably soared along with it. You showed up differently in your relationships. You were kinder and more gracious; you brought more optimism to the relational dynamic. Even in your work life, when you felt good about yourself that way, you probably had more energy, confidence, and enthusiasm, and you could push yourself a bit further toward excellence. But the most beautiful qualities of the soul are darkened and dampened when we are fighting an inner battle of self-sabotage, self-loathing, and destructive eating behaviors.

Each of us knows at some level when we're not heeding our bodies' need to be properly nourished or to get the healthy movement that every cell, system, and organ in our bodies depends on for life and longevity. We know deep down when we are being neglectful of or even abusive to our bodies. No matter how many books tell us to overlook this, at a gut-honest level, this reality is impossible to ignore. Why? Because our bodies are the only vehicles we have in which to express our souls and spirits. Tell me, could we possess any greater gift? We can't pretend that our health and fitness exist in a vacuum and that somehow they don't factor into the other important areas of our lives.

> Can you imagine what it might be like to have weight issues permanently eliminated from your life?

This is why it is vitally important to be connected to yourself at every level of your being. If you are carrying too much weight around, then whether you recognize it or not, the excess weight is taking a toll on your health and well-being. Ignoring your problems will never make them go away. Isn't it time to acknowledge the truth and make it your business to get to the bottom of the problem—to find out why you struggle with weight and what you can do to make yourself permanently fit and healthy?

Can you imagine what it might be like to have weight issues permanently eliminated from your life? Many people have lived with weight issues for so long they have begun to accept those issues as an integral part of their existence. It's sort of like planning for the seasons to come around: these folks get mentally pumped up for the day they're going to hit that same old diet program again so they don't face humiliation at the class reunion or the company trip to the beaches of Barbados. They buy the foods, do the exercise required, and then about six months after the event, they look in the mirror or step on the scales and say: "Oh no! What happened? It's all come back and then some!" And their weight-loss roller coaster gets stuck at the bottom again, facing a very large hill.

## Let's Talk about Forever

I have good news: that cycle can end forever! But the Skinny Life is not a quick-fix promise. We need to put that on the table right now. This is the rest of your life we are talking about, not just another weight-loss loop to try. I want to help you change *forever*. No more weight issues—ever!

> The part can never be well unless the whole is well.
> —Plato

If you are ready to begin the Skinny Life journey, then it's time to start connecting all the parts of you. When you start to acknowledge the connection between your mind, body, and spirit, then your life will get a whole lot better! Your zest for life, your fun-loving spirit, a smile that lights up your face, your compassion for others, your contribution each day to the people around you—all of these are enhanced and multiplied when you know you are honoring your body and yourself in your behaviors and choices.

The only way you can truly respect yourself and become the greatest expression of you is when you are living in a state of awareness and connection to all of the gifts that are yours in life, particularly your own body.

## Your Relationship with You

Successful management of your weight and health involves two important relationships: your relationship with food and your relationship with your own body.

As I began to work with my first Skinny Life test group, I was utterly amazed at what I found. Some of the women had been on thirty to forty diets during their lives! In our discussions, whenever I would ask how many of those diets were permanently successful, the answer was the same: *none*. What most of these women had endured was living on a weight-loss roller coaster that took them up and down but never let them off.

As we went deeper into our discussions, I found a common thread that I grew to understand was the key that unlocks the door to lasting health and fitness. What these women all had in common was that not one of them ever really believed, after using any of those programs, they were going to permanently be able to master their weight! In fact, most of them felt that the "fat" person would most certainly come out again. Often the women would save their "fat" clothes and cross their fingers that they could hold out a while longer this time. But they were convinced they were doomed to be overweight. When they became slimmer for a while, they felt like imposters in their own skin.

Think about it. How can you ever be successful at something

that deep in your heart you don't believe in? When you don't believe in yourself? Your beliefs about yourself come from a lifetime of experiences and feedback you've taken in from the world, plus the scenarios you imagine in your own mind. Each one of us walks around with a little bit of every experience inside of us, and those events and our impressions of them become the filters by which we process the rest of our lives. Those beliefs and filters create entrenched programs that run automatically at the subconscious level, whether you know it or not. If each day you carry around subtle beliefs that you are destined to be heavy, that you have inferior genes and an inferior constitution, then you are giving instructions to yourself at all levels to live out exactly that. How could you ever expect to be fit, slim, and healthy with a deeply embraced emotional and mental program that doesn't support it?

Most people have no idea how powerful their own beliefs are. Want the truth? Your inner beliefs could be more influential on the size and shape of your body than your genes are.

**Skinny Life Bottom Line:** Your inner beliefs could be more influential on the size and shape of your body than your genes are.

A study on the failure rates of weight-loss programs in America said, "The relationship between emotional eating and America's overweight problem does not seem to be addressed adequately by many weight management programs."[8] I created Skinny Life because I recognized that most weight-loss programs didn't address the connection between mental feedback and weight issues. This influence is the most important factor in success or failure in resolving weight issues.

## Develop Awareness

Rekindling our relationship with our bodies and food requires deliberate awareness. I can't tell you how many times I've seen people complain about their weight and health and then mindlessly eat a nutritionless doughnut or pastry. We all have destructive habits, emotions, and thoughts at levels of our minds that we're not in touch with. For many years my challenge to clients has been: Are you controlling your mind, or is your mind controlling you? We say we want to be healthier, be leaner, be more active, eat what truly nourishes our bodies, stay away from the foods that wreak havoc on our health, but when it comes to making the choice, those conscious thoughts seem to disappear and a subconscious force takes over. My work for many years has focused on breaking those destructive patterns and creating connected, positive thought and behavior patterns at all levels of consciousness.

The great news is that when you intervene in those destructive patterns on your own behalf, the benefits translate to all areas of your life. I worked with a client, Candace, helping her break out of years of destructive eating and body-image patterns. After beginning the Skinny Life lifestyle, she wrote to me:

> I can't believe it! I am not only loving and honoring myself more and making really good decisions about how I take care of my body from that place, I now have the courage to do things I never thought I could. I've wanted to leave this

job and a destructive relationship and start a new job in a more dynamic place for so long but was scared to make a move. Now I've decided to do it! I've found my new place in a new city, and I'm headed there to start a new life.

## Skinny Life Toolbox

### Be Honest with Yourself

Are you ready to get real about health and fitness? Then I want to ask you some tough questions. Answer them with raw honesty. Honesty with yourself is foundational for every positive change. It is human nature to try to fool ourselves or ignore the truth, especially when we know deep down that things need to change. I want you to remember this truth: the more you are willing to embrace change, the greater your chances for success in every area of life. Weight and health are no exception.

To move forward into Skinny Life freedom, start by answering these truth questions:

- Have you given up on staying healthy and fit and looking great?
- Are you taking the best care of your body?
- Are you truly happy with the shape you're in?
- Are you ignoring the truth about your physical energy and vitality?
- Are you ignoring the potential health consequences of neglecting your body's needs?

- Do you take care daily to do the best you can for yourself?
- Are there other areas of your life that feel out of control?
- Which area of your life is causing you the most stress right now?
- Which current situations cause you the most emotional instability?

You can never start to move in the right direction if you don't know where you are now. The answers to this honesty exercise will help you clearly and truthfully assess your current health and wellness. When you truly consider how you feel about your self-confidence, health, strength, vitality, and well-being, do you have what you want from life or are your answers telling you it's time to change things?

> The more you are willing to embrace change, the greater your chances for success in every area of life.

Use this exercise as a starting point on the path to something so much better. After you have answered the questions, reread your answers a second and third time. When you read the answers the third time, imagine them as the end of a mental and emotional place from which you are ready to move forward. If you're ready for real change that will lighten your spirit, mind, and body, then keep reading . . . your Skinny Life journey has already begun.

Starting today, make a decision to live with purpose and intention to honor your amazing body with each choice you make.

# Affirmations

I will apologize to myself for the times when
I've given up on myself.

I am ready to be fully honest about
the areas where I've neglected myself.

I am being truthful and authentic to myself about
the consequences of ignoring my health and fitness.

I will honestly acknowledge the times I feel out of control
in my life and take quiet time to reflect on why.

I am ready to recognize and admit the things
that cause me the most inner stress.

I will pay attention to feelings of emotional instability
I experience and then write down the circumstances
and events that trigger those feelings.

Being authentic and truthful with myself will
allow me to move forward in a clear direction
with my health and fitness.

I am ready to engage fully in staying healthy,
fit, and feeling great!

# 2

# The Amazing Body God Has Given You

Imagine that God showed up in your living room and said, "I hope you are enjoying and appreciating the gift of your body. I created it just for you. I gave it to you so you could express all you're meant to during this life on earth. Your body is a temple in which I can be with you and even dwell inside of you, if you invite me. Are you taking the best care of the body I've given to you?" How would you respond?

Would you start to sputter and stutter and try to explain why those fast-food cheeseburgers, fries, and sodas get you every time? How you're too busy or stressed out to pay attention to what is actually going into your body each day and what is being left out? Or maybe you'd admit that you're not sure how watching football or your favorite TV shows became more important than going on a walk or bike ride with your spouse, kids, or just peacefully by yourself.

I bring up this imagined scenario because before you can make major changes in your lifestyle and how you care for something, you need to understand its value. As far as your existence goes, your body is *the* vehicle, the only one, through which everything you experience called "life" happens.

> **Skinny Life Bottom Line:** Your body is *the* vehicle, the only one, through which everything you experience called "life" happens.

Let's consider the following aspects of life that depend on a healthy, well-cared-for body:

- how you experience God and your relationship with God
- how you experience your spousal or primary love relationship
- how you experience friendships
- how you bring life and nurture life—children, grand-children, nieces, nephews, siblings, parents
- how you express your creativity—arts, dance, music, architecture
- how you express your intelligence—science, language, mathematics
- how you make your contribution to the world via a career, a business, or philanthropy

*Everything* you ever think, do, become, or create will happen through your body. Do you see the importance of understanding the value of a fit, healthy, balanced body? Tragically, a lot of people don't until it's too late. Major diseases connected to obesity and overweight conditions include hypertension, heart disease, metabolic syndrome, diabetes, and even cancer.[1] You can decide today that you will not be someone who doesn't discover the value of her body until it's too late to change. Starting today, you can manage every destructive pattern you have related to the proper care and feeding of your most important asset.

## How Much Is Your Body Worth?

I want to share some information that caused me to bask in wonder when I first heard it years ago, as it still does today. Earl Nightingale, in his *Lead the Field* audio series, talks about the value of the human body, if you were to quantify it monetarily or scientifically. Nightingale says we are God's highest form of creation, yet most of us have no idea how much we are worth. If the electronic energy in the atoms of our bodies could be utilized, each of us could supply all of the electrical needs for an industrialized country for close to a week.

Scientists discovered that the atoms of the human body contain potential energy of eleven million kilowatt-hours per pound, which would make an average man or woman worth about $85 billion. The electrons in your body are not just particles of matter; they're waves of living energy that spread out in patterns of light. And as they move, they sing. With the right hearing device you would hear a great symphonic concert as these waves play and flow, merging with the waves of other matter.

These electrons in your body not only sing, but they also shine. If you stood in front of an infrared television camera in a dark room, the screen would show you from top to bottom as a glistening, radiating form. If you tried to reproduce your mind mechanically, you could spend billions of dollars, but you would still not be able to do it. And not only are you amazing and infinitely valuable, but you are unique. You're unlike any human being that's ever lived on earth, or ever will live on earth.[2]

Do you get it? There is nothing more valuable than the unique and beautiful body that God created just for you!

 **Skinny Life Bottom Line:** There is nothing more valuable than the unique and beautiful body that God created just for you!

So how do you treat your most valuable possession? Let me tell you what I've found in years of working with people about their health and well-being. We tend to treat our cars better . . . our houses better . . . and other people better than we treat our own bodies.

Why? There is no good answer. But here are some of the reasons I've uncovered as I've spoken to people about this very thing:

- We have the misguided idea that taking care of ourselves is selfish.
- We undervalue ourselves and begin to think others must be more important.
- We think we are shortchanging those we love if we don't give away every bit of ourselves to them.
- We fool ourselves into thinking that after we've helped everyone else first, then eventually we'll get to ourselves.

My friend, this is faulty thinking! Say out loud: "This needs to change now. I need to start treating my body better *today*."

 **Skinny Life Bottom Line:** Say out loud: "This needs to change now. I need to start treating my body better *today*."

## Meet Penny

Many people talk about respecting the sacredness of the gift of life. We protect our children, animals, and even unborn children. But do we remember to respect the sacredness of the gift of our own lives and bodies? At a subconscious level, so many of us marginalize or dismiss how special we are in this beautiful body through which we live, learn, and love.

My client Penny was the ultimate mother. She was smart, kind, loving, and patient with her children. She also worked a part-time job as a legal assistant. She was on top of everything. Nothing in her world slipped. Penny went out of her way to feed her kids very nutritious meals, and she loved decorating their rooms, sewing custom character pillows, and making them feel as though they lived in a special fantasyland. She tutored them each evening so they always got top grades in their classes, and they were never late to a music lesson or soccer practice.

Not only was Penny the ultimate mother, but she was also an outstanding wife. She talked about her husband's work as if it was more important than hers, even though people at her job swore they couldn't live without her great skill and efficiency. Penny came to me to be coached in organizational efficiency, essentially asking,

"How can I do a better job for everyone in my life?"

The tragedy? Penny couldn't see how neglectful and even abusive she was being to herself, particularly her physical body. While the kids ate healthy meals, Penny would catch up on calls and e-mails, then go flying out the door with peanut-butter crackers or a bagel for her own breakfast or dinner. Whenever she found a free moment to feed her starving self, she would resort to diving into the doughnuts at work or grabbing fast food on a five-to-ten-minute lunch "hour." As far as physical activity, forget it. Even during soccer practice or ballet lessons, instead of taking a walk, Penny caught up on work-related reading or writing a business proposal for her husband's business. (He liked the way she wrote them better than his hired staff.)

> What is always speaking silently is the body.
> —Norman Brown,
> psychologist and author

When Penny came back for our second appointment, I told her she'd hired me for the wrong reason. She was a little taken aback and then said, "I thought you could help coach me to more success in my life." I told her, "If you don't start realizing how special you are, how important you are, and how you are a sacred gift to the people around you, then your body is going to fall apart and your life will follow it."

Penny looked shocked for a moment and didn't say a word . . . and then the floodgates opened. As she hung her head and tears gushed, she admitted I was right. She didn't know how much longer she could last doing what she was doing: being everything to everyone. She confessed, "I feel like I don't exist sometimes." The more disgusted she felt with her own body the more she ignored it. "I feel like I live a thousand miles away from my own body. I'm afraid even to acknowledge my needs because I've ignored them for so long."

Penny was overweight, in terrible physical condition (in spite of having a husband who played tennis and stayed in great shape), and had lost all of the luster and shine in her face. She had been a pretty woman, but at some point she had made the decision, mostly at the subconscious level, to disconnect from her body's needs and dismiss herself as something that just wasn't that important. Ironically she was the sun and the moon to everyone in her family and at her workplace. None of them realized their sun was about to go dark if someone didn't intervene.

When you read Penny's story, do you see a little bit of Penny in yourself? Many people I've worked with find, when they start to examine their lives, that their health and well-being have become their lowest priorities. It's a realization that can make you feel desperately sad. Why? Because deep down, you know you deserve better. Somewhere inside, as you've put off your health and fitness needs again and again, you've made a silent promise to get back to that . . . someday. But someday hasn't come. How much time will you let go by before you start treating yourself better? How much of your life will you let slip by before you realize that this is the only life you've been given?

 **Skinny Life Bottom Line:** How much of your life will you let slip by before you realize that this is the only life you've been given?

God made your body with a perfect accounting system. No matter how much we delude ourselves into thinking poor eating choices and a lack of healthy active movement will somehow reconcile themselves in the end, our body's cells and systems can't be fooled. If you think of your body and health like a bank account—with poor eating and sedentary habits being debits, and wholesome foods and vital exercise being deposits or credits—then you understand that you can't keep writing checks and taking withdrawals without replenishing your account with new cash deposits. Just like you could end up financially bankrupt by running your financial life that way, you could end up bankrupting your own health.

With Penny, we had to start with the bottom-line truth that "someday" may never come, especially if she continued to put aside her own health and fitness for everything else. Today is what matters. Each day in its twenty-four-hour fullness.

## Penny's Progress

Out of each of those big twenty-four-hour days that were rolling by, I asked Penny to pick two forty-five-minute segments where she would focus only on her health and fitness no matter what! One segment would involve healthy movement and the other would include healthy eating. She could use one section of time for walking, bike riding, taking a dance class, or doing some gentle weight lifting while listening to her favorite music. Then she could dedicate the other segment of time to thinking about her nutrition, planning meals in advance, and shopping for much healthier food and snacks.

Amazingly, she found that the world didn't fall apart in that ninety minutes without her! She still had twenty-two and a half hours each day to care for her family, work, eat, and sleep. Penny's husband started commenting that she seemed happier, more relaxed, and a lot more fun. Her kids seemed to enjoy more independent time without their mom hovering nearby to take care of every little thing. At work they thought it was awesome that she was doing more for herself. In fact, others got on board, so lunchtime walks became the new thing.

## Skinny Life Toolbox

### Make Photo Reminders

Gather photos of yourself with your parents, children, friends, and others who are important to you. Also get one photo of just you with your favorite spiritual picture or Scripture verse next to it. Then tape these pictures to a piece of paper and write next to each one:

- *My greatest health and fitness are important to my husband because* (list all of the reasons)
- *My greatest health and fitness are important to my children because* (list all of the reasons)
- *My greatest health and fitness are important to my job because* (list all of the reasons)
- *My greatest health and fitness are important to God and me because I'm here to be the greatest expression of me possible.*

Each morning, spend five minutes of quiet time going through those photos and reminders.

# Affirmations

I'm ready to pay attention to my priorities and notice
immediately when I am putting myself last.

I recognize that my behaviors each hour and
each day become a lifetime of behavioral patterns.

Each day is important to my health and fitness.
I do not put it off until tomorrow.

My health and fitness are vitally important
to me and to all those I love.

I am here on this earth to be
the greatest expression of me!

# 3

# Stop Weighing and Worrying

Once you've acknowledged the wonder of the body God gave you, the next step in your Skinny Life challenge is stop weighing and worrying! Remember, the Skinny Life journey begins in your mind, and part of that is getting rid of the mind tricks that play out when you do things like weighing and worrying.

In other words, throw away your scales and stop counting calories! *What could that possibly mean?* you may wonder. *That's the basis of almost every weight-loss program! How will I measure my success if I'm not counting calories and pounds?*

 **Skinny Life Bottom Line:** Throw away your scales and stop counting calories!

People are often surprised when I say, "Don't weigh yourself and don't bother to count calories." It goes against everything they've ever thought or been taught about how they need to lose

35

weight. The reason I teach this is because when we start counting, we start measuring—and, more often than not, we perceive we've fallen short of our goal and feel we have failed. We have assigned a specific number on the scale as *the* determination of whether we're getting healthy.

Many people live and die by the readout on their scales, but they are often disconnected from the way their bodies truly interact with food, movement or a lack of it, and the emotional strongholds their life events hold over their health and fitness. As a result, lasting weight loss is hampered.

The problem with the number on the scale is that it provides limited information about our overall health and fitness. The scale doesn't tell the whole story. If the number isn't what we think it's supposed to be, then it starts a psychological cascade of negative thoughts that create identity-forming statements: "I'm fat." "I can't get thin." "I will never get on top of this problem." "I'm blowing it." "Weight loss is impossible for me."

The truth is, those thoughts are the most important influence on your permanent fitness and health. They set up your identity, and actions and habits follow.

 **Skinny Life Bottom Line:** The scale doesn't tell the whole story.

This is a self-limiting cycle that we need to get rid of forever. The Skinny Life isn't about measuring up. Stepping on the scales each day can give you an unnecessary psychological trip that isn't helpful in living masterfully with your health and weight.

## The Problem with Scales

Erin would not drink water throughout the day because she claimed it gave her "water weight." When she drank six or seven glasses of water a day and then stepped on the scale, she weighed more than she had that morning. So Erin started drastically cutting back her water consumption, thinking it would help with her weight. But it didn't help anything. She began to have health issues, including kidney stones and intestinal dysfunction, because her body became water deficient.

Our amazing bodies need water—lots of it! Water cleanses all of our organs, including intestines, kidneys, and skin. It lowers your blood pressure, enhances your brain function, and helps give you a full feeling that can help you avoid overeating.

Dr. Howard Flaks, a bariatric physician who has been treating famous people in Beverly Hills for over thirty years, says that drinking water is likely one of the most important parts of successful weight loss. There are many reasons for this. First, water cleanses the liver, which is the organ of fat breakdown. Second, it prevents baggy skin resulting from weight loss by toning up the skin's elasticity. And finally, drinking more water helps get rid of the by-product of fat metabolism.

Drinking ten to twelve cups of water (eighty to ninety-six ounces) a day is *very* beneficial in maintaining a healthy weight. In fact, I've found with my clients that good water drinkers have a much easier time mastering their weight and health. A recent study published in the *Journal of Clinical Endocrinology and Metabolism* supports my observation. The study found that drinking five hundred milliliters of water daily increases metabolic rate by 30 percent in both men and in women. The metabolic rate began to increase within ten minutes after the water drinking, and the effect was sustained for more than an hour. That's because it takes energy to process water and that energy output burns calories and raises metabolism. They concluded that by *increasing* daily water consumption by a little more than six cups, energy expenditure would increase by 17,400 calories per year, the energy content of 5.6 pounds of adipose (fat) tissue! You literally can start to drink off the fat![1]

> The muscle tissue you begin to put on will act like your own personal fat-burning furnace.

After a few of our sessions, Erin finally realized that water was not an enemy. She discovered through the Skinny Life program that natural teas act as a safe, healthy diuretic to eliminate excess water weight plus provide her body with cancer-fighting chemicals that are naturally present in green, white, and black teas.

You can see how weighing yourself all of the time could be confusing and discouraging, because your body is going through various metabolic processes throughout the day and some of the healthier things you are doing could throw the numbers off temporarily. Believe me, when you start to eat right and increase your movement each day, consuming an appropriate amount of water to keep hydrated, you will notice right away how differently your clothes fit, how you look in the mirror, and most important, how much better you feel. The numbers that pop up on your scale can be deceiving, particularly because muscle weighs more than fat.

As you start to lose fat and replace it with healthy muscle, at certain points of your journey you might get discouraged because the scales don't show lower numbers, yet you are looking better, feeling better, and getting much healthier. A pound of fat takes up more space than a pound of muscle. But the beautiful muscle tissue you begin to put on will act like your own personal fat-burning furnace, raising your metabolism and helping you look leaner and feel stronger.

As the Skinny Life becomes your lifestyle, you will begin to recognize foods by their value, including energy (sometimes quantified by calories) and the way they interact with your natural body systems. Eating right and being fit will become a normal way of life for you.

## Scales Can Block Reconnecting to Yourself

If you rely solely on physical measurements, such as scale readouts, to judge how well you are changing your habits and losing weight, then you may miss the vital objective to mastering health: reconnecting to yourself.

Here at the beginning of your Skinny Life journey, you've probably recognized that you've been disconnected from your body and your health for a while. But when you start to connect, you'll notice a lot of great things!

- You'll start to feel excited and hopeful that there's a better life waiting for you.
- You'll start to feel less worried and less afraid.
- Best of all, you'll begin to feel a calm sense of control.

Skinny Lifers feel a greater sense of purpose and peace in every area of their lives, even after only a couple of months. For many, the Skinny Life lifestyle choice was the most empowering decision they'd ever made on their own behalf. Few things in life are of greater value than your physical health and well-being. As we go deeper into this journey, that will become more and more apparent.

I've found time and again when clients aren't connected to their bodies and health, they feel out of control in other areas of their lives. It's a terrible way to live. But the good news is all of that can begin to change right here and now. If you want to keep a scale, fine—but don't let it be the final arbiter of how well you are doing. Instead, focus on interconnection of your mind and body. I'll show you how.

## Meet Kristy

My client Kristy had become lethargic about herself, her life, and her work, all because she didn't like the way weight had been creeping up on her. She felt disgusted with her body and herself, and at the same time, nothing in her life seemed to be working very well. She started to dread work and social engagements, and even her marriage was on shaky ground.

By the time she found Skinny Life, Kristy had become discouraged and disconnected from her life. She wasn't sure how she was feeling about the stress at work or if she really even *wanted* to be doing the sales and marketing that had been her career for so many years. Sales were slipping as her attitude plummeted, creating even more pressure and financial stress at home. As those emotions played out, Kristy stopped paying attention to what she was eating because she was so preoccupied with what her next move would be.

When she came to me she said, "I feel so out of touch with myself, what I want, and how to get it." Know the feeling? I helped her intervene in the cycle by starting out with some truth questions (see chapter 1). When she answered those, she immediately started connecting the dots. It became clear that she needed to start a Skinny Life journey that would reconnect her to her amazing body so she could address all the parts of her life she was unhappy about. She realized through her truth process that she had gotten into a destructive pattern of stepping on the scale each day, feeling worse about herself and totally lost about how to change those numbers, and then feeling even more disconnected from herself and her own happiness. We started out not by focusing on numbers on a scale, but by reconnecting to the things she'd lost touch with that brought joy *and* health and fitness to her life.

Kristy remembered that she had previously enjoyed jogging in a big park near her home; in fact, for years she'd done it as often as four or five times weekly. She hadn't done that in over a year, and she realized that returning to some kind of active movement that she loved was a beneficial next step. When she began to take this time for herself, it freed her mind to focus on what she really wanted from her life and what didn't fit into that picture.

Kristy thought she might enjoy volunteering in the youth ministry at her church, but in the past year, there had never seemed to be time. Each time she went to the park again, with the fresh air moving through her, she felt she was getting back in touch with God and the special gifts he had given her. Kristy had already intervened in a loving, positive way with a couple of teenagers in her younger cousin's peer group. That effort made her feel happier and more fulfilled than anything she had ever done. When she helped these young people feel safe and talked with them about their lives and problems, the teens responded remarkably well to her easy-going, loving counsel.

As Kristy experimented further with healthy activity and efforts, she began to get clearer in her intentions and in honoring her own body, respecting that she had a purpose and she needed to stay healthy and fit to fulfill it.

> The weight she began to lose and the inches that started to peel off were just a by-product of living a healthy, connected life.

With Skinny Life guidance, she started getting better nutrition with supplements and health shakes on those busy days when she couldn't eat. She became more skillful at planning snacks and meals that would fuel her body and not burden it with empty calories. When her snacks and quick meals changed from a sugary muffin or slice of pizza to avocados, carrots, celery, almonds, yogurt, tuna, chicken, or a protein shake, Kristy started feeling a lot less cranky with her husband—plus, she had much more energy for the work ahead of her each day! Work started feeling like a more positive place. And when she finally took the leap and officially got involved in youth group activities, she started picking up business from the parents of the teens she worked with because they were so thankful she had such a kind, authentic, straightforward personality that blessed their kids' lives.

Kristy's energy and enthusiasm went up, her sales rose, and her relationship with her husband became better than it had been in five years. All the areas of her life started improving when she began reconnecting to herself through the Skinny Life process. The weight she began to lose and the inches that started to peel off were just a by-product of living a healthy, connected life.

## Look at Food Truthfully

Think for a minute about what happens when you feel your worst about yourself and your body. What leads up to it? Are you making eating decisions based on circumstances around you? Does the scale readout provoke feelings of defeat? Or are you a random eater? In other words, when Ethan gets doughnuts for the office every morning, do you go ahead and eat them because . . . uh . . . they're sitting there? Is that a good reason to eat something?

A doughnut is made of starch, which has been stripped of its fiber and food value, plus some white bleached sugar, and fats that aren't good for your body. If you saw those ingredients sitting on the counter with a description of the effect each ingredient has on your body, would you stuff them into your mouth? Most people don't look at food for what it really is. We're totally disconnected from what's going into our mouths. If only our cells could talk to us, they might be saying, "Please stop! Enough already! I can't take much more of this."

**Skinny Life Bottom Line:** Most people don't look at food for what it really is. We're totally disconnected from what's going into our mouths.

One of the problems we face as a society is that instead of toiling for our food and taking time to prepare it, as we had to historically, food is now everywhere all the time, whether we need it or not. Remember when we got to have cupcakes only on our birthdays or special occasions? Now cupcake shops are on every third corner in just about every major city in the United States. And these are giant cupcakes loaded with sugary frosting! Even in developing countries, where starvation used to be the problem, now a bigger problem looms. Diabetes is becoming a global burden, as many food products made with trans fats and refined sugars and flours have been made cheaper and more available.

These foods do more harm than good. The mitochondria in our bodies are programmed to survive and thrive longer and stronger with periods of fasting and low calorie consumption, rather than the overload of poor-quality, even toxic foods that we are now consuming.

My husband and I do a speaking tour through China several times a year. Lately I've noticed some drastic changes there that don't bode well for the Chinese people. Fewer people are riding bicycles or walking. As we move through the streets of Shanghai now, it appears the number of bike riders through whom we've always had to navigate is less than half what it was three or four years ago. More people are driving cars. The air is so polluted now that fewer people go outside to exercise.

In 1980 less than 1 percent of the adult Chinese population was diabetic. One study estimated that figure is to be around 12 percent in 2010. In fact, one in every three diabetic persons in the world is Chinese.[2] Food abundance and physical inactivity are causing a type

2 diabetes epidemic![3] In September 2013, the most comprehensive survey ever conducted in China, which was published by the American Medical Association, revealed 114 million Chinese—a population the size of Mexico's—now have the disease.[4]

Businessmen who grew up surrounded by famine and violent political campaigns are now becoming rich off of China's growth. They want a better life, but unfortunately the spoils of that life are creating an obese society. The government fears that the problems associated with obesity could bankrupt the country's healthcare system.[5]

You may wonder what China's issues have to do with you. Unfortunately, much of what is considered food in our modern society is devoid of nutrition and full of empty calories that end up taking a great toll on our health and energy rather than nourishing us. You and I also live in a prosperous country in which food quality is often lacking.

You see, rather than weighing and measuring ourselves, we need to focus on the quality and content of the foods we eat. When given the right vegetables, fruits, non-GMO whole grains (more on this in chapter 11), and forms of lean proteins in reasonable amounts, your body is truly fueled and it *knows* it. These foods are full of complex nutrients and micronutrients, enzymes, fiber, and protein. When you eat them, your body digests and processes them naturally so the cells are nourished and the body *and* appetite are satisfied.

It's important to start seeing food for what it is when beginning the Skinny Life journey. Most of the time when we get into bad eating habits, we are associating those junk foods with some kind of positive feeling. Look at the way TV commercials seduce you into thinking that cola will make you more giving and connected to humanity and that beer drinking will make you sexy and thin. Really? And consider those times when you felt bad and Grandma made you a double hot fudge sundae to forget how mean those kids treated you. You get where I'm going? Our hidden beliefs and feelings about the foods we shouldn't be eating cause us to run to them for emotional soothing.

In the Skinny Life journey, we will break those hidden feelings and belief triggers about foods by going straight to the foods and straightening our thoughts and feelings about them. This is a great beginning step for our new food relationships. I'm going to ask you to become a bit of an explorer on this one, but with all the resources available at your fingertips online, it should be easy and enlightening.

## Skinny Life Toolbox

### "What's Inside" Food Exercise

Make a list of your top five favorite junk foods, and underneath each item write what it is made of. For instance:

- *Doughnuts*
  White, fiberless starch that turns into sugar; white, bleached sugar that has no food value; shortening or lard, which is fat that accumulates around the organs and wreaks havoc in the body.

- *Packaged cookies*

  White sugar with no food value; white flour that turns into sugar; hydrogenated or partially hydrogenated vegetable oil to preserve for long shelf life, which are very bad for the body; high fructose corn syrup, which is just as bad as white sugar, maybe worse.

- *Fast-food french fries*

  Potato deep-fried so most of its nutrition is cooked out; soaked with hydrogenated fats or trans fats, which are very bad in the body.

- *Cola*

  High fructose corn syrup (diabetes causer), caffeine (too much not good), and phosphoric acid (leeches the calcium from your bones), flavorings.

- *White bagel*

  White flour that turns to sugar in the body, with double gluten in it.

Now add to the list of your favorite junk foods, five healthy alternatives to those snacks and the ingredients in those. For example:

- *Whole grain brown rice cakes with light cream cheese*

  Whole, healthy grain with fiber and nutrition still intact, balanced with a boost of natural protein and healthy fat.

- *Apple slices dipped in natural peanut butter*

  Natural, nutritious fruit filled with vitamins, great fiber, natural sugars, and non-hydrogenated healthy nut butter for a bit of healthy fat/protein combo.

- *Baked veggie chips with two tablespoons low-fat sour cream onion dip*
  Baked vegetable ingredients so nutrition is still there, with a healthy bit of protein (in the sour cream) to dip with.
- *Small bowl of cherry tomatoes with mozzarella cheese balls*
  Nutritious veggie loaded with natural vitamins, enzymes, good source of protein, and healthy fat balance.
- *Celery with flavored hummus*
  Healthy veggie, vitamins, enzymes, raw nutrition, with very healthy garbanzo bean dip. Nice combination of protein with some healthy fat (olive oil in the hummus).

The point of this exercise is to get in the habit of seeing food for what it really is and not to use foods to bridge emotional needs. Food can and should be enjoyed, but the primary purpose of eating is nourishment, not mindless destruction of the body. When you focus on what is really contained in the food and not the exterior image of it, you begin to see how those ingredients relate to your body, instead of disconnecting from that truth. Focus on the quality (or lack of it) in every single food that goes in your mouth. This is a much more productive focus than counting numbers on a scale.

As you continue forward in your Skinny Life journey, learning the philosophy and the techniques of healthy eating and living, you will begin to understand that weighing and worrying are best left in the past. The scale is no longer necessary. After you've had a few months of practice, you can weigh yourself every once in a while just for fun. But it won't be because you are afraid of what the numbers might say. It will be out of mild curiosity. You'll already know how well you're treating yourself, how your Skinny Life is working, and how great you feel.

I'm asking you to make a big paradigm shift by measuring your healthy success in new ways, because that is the only method by which weight mastery becomes permanent, and your health and fitness become completely natural. Stick with me. You *can* do this.

# Affirmations

I am letting go of my weighing and worrying habits.

I am focusing on the quality of my life and
the things that bring me joy.

When I connect to joyful things,
I am connecting to and understanding myself better.

I am making it my business to know
what's in the foods I eat.

I am focusing on eating better-quality foods and
leaving bad foods behind.

Unhealthy, destructive foods don't deserve
a place in my body.

# 4

# Weight and Health Issues
# Start in Your Mind

Scientists have told us again and again that we use less than 10 percent of our brains' potential. Part of the reason for this is that the largest area of our minds is the subconscious. This is the area where every bit of the history of our lives resides. Our experiences and our perceptions of those experiences are held inside this giant storage tank commonly referred to as the subconscious mind.

Imagine there is an invisible door at the bottom of our conscious mind, and we can open the door and peer inside. If that were true, we would find a vast collection of beliefs, ideas, and even the answers to the very issues that trouble us the most. One of the techniques I use with my clients is guided meditation. This technique relaxes the conscious mind so that we naturally drop into a slower-brain-wave state, opening up the parts of the brain where things have stayed hidden from our conscious reach. Now when I talk about meditation, I am not referring to any specific religious or spiritual tradition. I'm simply referring to a calm, reflective state of mind that is not barraged by a million thoughts of what we should be doing.

If we are ruminating over negative things about ourselves, we could be off track from the path God meant for us. So much of our negative automatic thinking is done at a subconscious level. This is why it is so important to deliberately quiet our minds to use our subconscious resources in an affirming, positive way on our own behalf, rather than letting random experiences take charge of our thoughts and control our actions or lack of constructive action.

The more we are able to access this part of ourselves, the more we begin to uncover buried programming that has been acting as self-sabotage.

You can probably relate to this when you think back on how many times you have made a resolution, set a goal, or wanted to make a major change. You meant well, you thought for sure you could do it, and you made up your mind and got started . . . but then something happened. You found yourself completely off track. Suddenly you are on the self-sabotage detour. The frustrating thing about these off-road pathways is that they're often hidden from your up-front, conscious view. They throw you off and you don't even know how it happened. But you do know that each time it happens you feel more powerless and discouraged about ever accomplishing your health and weight goals.

How do we get in touch with those painful self-sabotage programs that keep us from being our best?

## Use Silence to Engage Your Subconscious

This busy world in which we live gives us very little time away from the noise and clutter of our conscious minds. Our brains are constantly besieged with input: lists of what we must get done, things we're worried about, incessant e-mails, phone calls, and texts. . . . Wow! Do you ever think that if God is trying to communicate with us, he might be a bit frustrated? He is trying to get our attention through all of this stuff we fill our lives with, but to do that he needs us to be more available without the chaos.

That is why one of the tools I teach clients to use is silence. One of the most helpful things about guided meditation is that it allows you to quiet your mind. Only a quiet mind is receptive to new learning, new programming, and, especially important, new messages from God—as well as revealing where we begin to self-sabotage.

## Skinny Life Toolbox

### Silence Meditation

I'm going to share one of my favorite simple silence meditations. This exercise helps me feel closer to God and reconnects me to my greatest sense of purpose in life. When you reconnect to your life purpose, you'll find that loving and respecting yourself comes more easily. So does making choices that reflect that self-love and self-respect. Read this exercise through fully, then sit quietly (preferably with your eyes closed) to practice it.

Take a deep breath. As you inhale imagine that you are scooping up all negativity from every cell of your body and mind, and then imagine letting it go on your exhale. Do this same "scooping and letting go" breath three times. Then settle quietly into noticing your breath, and just breathe normally. Next begin to imagine a gentle white light, filled with love, starting at the top of your head and then ever so slowly going down through your face, cheekbones, jaw, neck, down your back, through all your vertebrae, and continuing down through your lower back, hips, legs, feet, and pushing any remaining negativity out the bottoms of your feet. Do this very slowly and really imagine how soothing it feels.

Before I begin this meditation exercise, I like to say a simple prayer to God, like, "Show me how to live my very best life," or "Help me honor myself and my precious body that you have given to me." You can use these or other prayer statements that would be meaningful to you, as this is a very personal experience. For me, bringing God into the experience makes it much more powerful and meaningful.

When you're through with your silence meditation, try to journal any thoughts, reflections, or breakthroughs that come to you. These will become some of your stepping-stones on the journey to the new you.

## Change Starts in the Mind

When we seek to change anything significant in our lives, we must start with the mind and mental programming, because as our lives play out, the mind is the director of everything we do, everything we have become, and everything we will become. So . . . how powerful *is* your mind in determining the way your body functions, the way you function, and the way your world functions?

 **Skinny Life Bottom Line:** The mind is the director of everything we do and everything we will become.

When you were growing up, your mind was in a constant learning state. From the time you were a baby, the people around you and the things happening in your environment fed your mind. The events, experiences, and ideas that your young brain absorbed shaped your beliefs, attitudes, and habits before you even knew it was happening. The problem, sometimes, is that those beliefs and attitudes often came from people who had flaws in their own beliefs and attitudes. As a result, often what you downloaded from their thoughts to your thoughts included insecurities, shame, and limitations that they had dealt with. Since your young, developing mind was like a sponge, you consumed everything that came in—and some of it wasn't so good.

Nonetheless, it all came together to form the thought and belief patterns that you began to process the rest of your life by. Your mind is infinitely powerful and is the reference center for everything you think and do.

## Have You Developed a Fat Identity?

Many people who have developed a "fat identity" or live with fears of being overweight grew up with relatives who began conveying their own beliefs and fears about their bodies to them at a very young age. It might have been a comment from a well-meaning grandma who blurted out at a family picnic, "Don't let her keep eating that stuff or she'll end up with my giant thighs." I have a client who remembers hearing her father tell her mother when he thought she was out of earshot, "I don't think she'll ever get a date to the prom until she loses all of that chubbiness. She just can't seem to stay away from doughnuts and cookies." Guess what? She didn't get a date to the high school prom and she did develop an addiction to junk foods.

Not surprisingly, a lot of these experiences from our youth become self-fulfilling prophecies, especially when they came from people we loved and trusted. The seed was set in our subconscious mind and it continued to grow with every experience that reinforced the message, until we ended up with a destructive belief pattern. This pattern tells us we're doomed to a life of weight problems, and consequently, addictive food behaviors start to rule.

## Skinny Life Toolbox

### Discover Your Core Beliefs

Let's try an exercise to reveal your core beliefs. First, get present to yourself. Shut out every other thought for now. Sit quietly in a private place and think about the words you tell yourself about your body image. I suggest writing them down in a journal. I've worked with people who have joked about their weight issues and acted publicly like they're no big deal. When we explored more deeply and honestly, though, the pain, fear, and insecurity around their body image was quite raw. Be very honest with yourself, because often we don't want to acknowledge our real feelings even to ourselves because it can open up our vulnerabilities.

- What are your *real* beliefs about the body God gave you, even the beliefs you have never expressed before?
- Do you carry any silent pain or worries about your body image and act like everything is okay when it's not what you really feel?
- How early did any negative beliefs about your body start? What is your earliest memory associated with a negative body image?
- What are your beliefs about food? Do you connect to how it supports life, or do you disconnect from the effect that foods have on your body?
- Did someone in your past project a negative image about your body that you are now afraid will become true?
- What other experiences in your past have reinforced a negative body image or fears of getting fat?
- Do you feel numb sometimes when you eat or do you eat to numb your feelings?
- Do you have the habit of disconnecting from your feelings rather than exploring them?
- In the past, have you felt there was no real solution to your weight issues? How did this belief affect your actions?
- Do you prefer to ignore what's important because it feels daunting?
- Do you believe that being fit, healthy, and slim is something you deserve? Something you can accomplish?

This exercise can be very helpful in helping you see the people, circumstances, and experiences that contributed to the beginning of a cycle of self-sabotage or accepting a "fat identity," so that you can release it for good.

## What Is Psychological Reversal?

You've noticed that each chapter concludes with affirmations you can use to keep focused and positive in your pursuit of health. In fact, these affirmation and commitment statements are structured to help you get past psychological reversal. What's that? Psychological reversal is a subconscious condition of self-sabotage.

> Psychological reversal is a subconscious condition of self-sabotage.

How do you know if you have been functioning in this state? Think back through the years. Do you notice that often, just as you have been in the process of achieving or attaining something you wanted, you somehow managed to spoil it? In psychological reversal, your subconscious mind is set on thwarting your successes, therefore success is harder to attain and sustain. I have worked with several clients who were psychologically reversed, including:

- A thirty-five-year-old man had gone from rags to riches and attained great financial success only to consistently lose his fortune with poor investments.
- A teenage girl easily made good friends but then ended up antagonizing them and driving them away.
- A very nice woman wanted desperately to have a loving

marital relationship but would catch herself criticizing and picking fights with her husband.

• A beautiful woman, a model and actress, found that every time she got her dream job, she starting eating junk food uncontrollably. She lost several opportunities that could have thrust her into the national limelight.

When people with psychological reversal experience positive situations, they don't trust that good times will last, so they begin to misbehave or act out just when things are getting good. By doing so they inadvertently undermine their own success.

## The Placebo Effect and the Power of Belief

I suspect that you've heard of the placebo effect, but let me give you my own definition if you haven't. The placebo effect is a beneficial effect produced when a placebo drug or treatment is given that cannot be attributed to the drug or treatment itself, and must therefore be due to the patient's belief in the treatment.

A famous study published by the *New England Journal of Medicine* was based on surgery performed by Dr. Bruce Moseley, an orthopedic surgeon. Dr. Moseley designed a randomized, double-blind, placebo-controlled clinical trial. In the study, the doctor performed knee surgery on one group. On the other group, he crafted a fake surgery where patients were sedated and three incisions were made into the skin and then sewn back up so it looked identical to the real surgery. One-third of the group who got the actual surgery experienced a resolution of their knee issues. The shocker? Patients who had gotten the "fake" surgery had the *same* results, which left researchers stunned. There was even a point in the study where the fake-surgery patients reported less knee pain than those who had experienced the real procedure, probably because they didn't have to heal from the deeper trauma of actual surgery.[1]

Here are just a few more documented cases of placebo experiments that resulted in amazing findings:

- People suffering from Irritable Bowel Syndrome (IBS) received sham acupuncture procedures, in which practitioners used needles that retracted back into the handles and didn't penetrate the patient's skin. An amazing 44 percent of patients reported relief from their IBS symptoms.[2]
- Patients with asthma said they felt 46 percent better after fake acupuncture and 45 percent better after fake inhaler treatment—just about even with the 50 percent who felt better after getting the real asthma treatment.[3]
- A patient was told she was getting a breakthrough medicine that promised a cure for her severe nausea and vomiting. Remarkably, within twenty minutes of ingesting the drug, the nausea subsided completely. The doctors had actually given her ipecac, a remedy that causes vomiting![4]

The science about the placebo effect is staggering. Hundreds of studies have been published about the placebo effect in healing and/or curing people of all kinds of ailments and diseases. This is important for us to pay attention to when it comes to our weight mastery journey.

We're conditioned to trust only things we can see, touch, and hold. Like pills. Like a treatment a doctor administers to us. But in all of these cases, it wasn't the pills or treatment that benefited the patient. It was a person's *belief* that created the positive result. Only the belief had power, and the belief had so much power that healing took place. Cures happened. People felt their symptoms disappear.

In the same way, your inner beliefs about weight loss and health also control your programs and habits. Sometimes those beliefs exist at the subconscious level. In other words, they could be running the show, but you don't even know they're there. New awareness and connection to yourself at deeper levels will help you begin a new kind of relationship with yourself. A change in your beliefs will then begin to happen.

## What Else Gets in the Way?

Could it be that your body is taking direction from possibly erroneous beliefs in your mind? Could it be that hidden programs that formed in your brain from the time you were a child are the very things that are keeping you from becoming the best you in your health and fitness? The evidence says yes!

Your mind constantly circulates thought patterns and beliefs that are either helping you or hurting you in every major area of your life, whether it's your weight and fitness, fulfilling relationships, or your confidence in your ability to have a creative and successful career. If you have spent much of your life struggling to get the things you desire but never quite reaching them, you can be sure that you're carrying around belief patterns that are keeping you engaged in that battle. Your own buried beliefs will continue to sabotage your success until you address them. (We'll talk about this more in the next chapter.)

 **Skinny Life Bottom Line:** Your own buried beliefs will continue to sabotage your success until you address them.

Because your habits are formed by your thought patterns, if you are going to change your habits, then you are going to have to start by changing the thought patterns in your mind that are keeping those habits alive! Many people have come to me with a clear sense that something is going on within their minds that they can't seem to control. Thoughts and actions are happening, but not the way they want them to be happening.

## Meet Vickie

When Vickie came to me she didn't know what was wrong with her. She wanted to feel good about herself and her body, but no matter how much she dieted or tried new weight-loss programs, her negative feelings about herself never changed. Whether she was at her ideal weight or back to being heavier again, she couldn't get rid of the nagging sense that she couldn't get it right when it came to her weight and health.

When I helped her explore her belief patterns, she discovered that throughout her childhood, mealtime conversations frequently included admonitions about how you should watch it or you would get fat. Her mother and aunts were obsessed with their fear of being fat. Going back to her memories of being a young girl, she couldn't remember a time she didn't feel anxious or worried about becoming fat. As a result, her belief pattern was that she couldn't enjoy foods and she should be afraid of eating no matter what.

"Until Skinny Life came along," she told me, "I didn't think it was okay to enjoy food. Food was an enemy that could always come back and conquer me. Now I respect and love myself and make my eating choices from a loving place of doing good for myself. It's easy to have the weight come off when you're making choices from a good place and not silently beating yourself up all the time."

Keep in mind that a belief is nothing more than a chronic pattern of thought. You have the ability, if you try even a little bit, to begin a new thought pattern, to tell yourself a new story. As we move forward, you will be able to change what you are manifesting in your health and fitness by recognizing all that you no longer want, and then visualizing the health and lifestyle you desire. I'll show you how to continue to layer your intentions and attention, so that you develop a chronic pattern of thought that supports your greatest vision of yourself!

# Affirmations

I recognize that my belief patterns are just habits
and they can be changed.

I am noticing my own belief patterns that turn
into self-sabotage.

I notice when negative projections of
my body creep up from my past.

I notice the people who might have projected their fears
and negative body image onto me, but I forgive them
and release the fear and negative images.

I picture a healthy, fit me every day, throughout the day.

My image of myself is changing positively
and permanently.

My belief patterns are changing to support
my healthy, fit habits.

Part Two

# A New Way of Looking at Weight and You

## 5

# Pain and Punishment Are Out; Love and Respect Are In

Why are we so mean to ourselves? I know that's a blunt question, but it's an important one. As I've worked with people over the years, it's become evident that most people carry around some negative subconscious programming:

- I am not worthy.
- I am not good enough.
- I'm not lovable.
- I don't deserve the best life has to offer.
- I deserve to be punished.

One of the most transformational components of the Skinny Life happens when people become aware of how hard they are on themselves. I'm always amazed when I sit with clients, gathering intake information from them, and they make statements like these:

- I can't eat right because it takes too much time to figure it out and I don't have an extra minute in my day.
- I have to take care of my kids. I don't have a half hour for me.
- My husband wants me to be there when he gets home and he's too tired to help with the kids, so I can't get to a Zumba class.
- I can't spend the money on supplements that would keep me healthy because my kids wouldn't have mall money.
- I have to provide for my family and help my wife when I get home, so there's not an extra hour for me to go for a jog.
- I can't leave the office because I have too much to do, so I eat whatever junk food is there.
- I can't afford to buy healthy food. It's too expensive.

It's surprising to me how little people will do to honor, feed, and care for their own bodies! We saw this in chapter 2 with my client Penny. These folks will give all of their time and energy to their kids, their jobs, their spouses, and the friends who need them, but often they will not save one bit of time or money to do something good for themselves.

Why do we feel as if we must martyr ourselves so everyone else can be okay? Why do we feel we must give every ounce of our time, energy, and devotion to others, but never to ourselves? In God's eyes, aren't we his children too? We seem to forget that and when we do, it can result in self-destructive behaviors that wreak havoc in our health, which then affects all the other important areas of our lives.

Ignoring and dishonoring yourself and your own body can set off a destructive cascade of events that looks something like this story of another client of mine.

## Meet David

David is one of the most lovable, precious men I've ever met. He has five children and a devoted wife he's been married to since he was a young man. David has worked in the media and direct marketing business for many years, leading and guiding different teams within companies to great success. If you asked his current employer, he would say his company wouldn't be where it is today without David's brilliant marketing strategies and unwavering leadership. David habitually works all day without a break and into the late hours of the night, directing teams around the world, solving countless problems, only to get up in the wee hours of the following morning to start again. He rarely takes the time to eat a healthy meal and instead surrounds himself with snack foods to push through the day.

So what's the problem here? David weighs in at 480 pounds! After David and I met through a business connection and I started sharing my Skinny Life philosophy and program with him, he came to me confidentially and said, "I know you have the true answer to my weight issues. This is a darkness I've suffered with for years. I've done all kinds of pills, powders, and diets my whole life, but Crystal, you are exactly right. The real problem is in my subconscious mind, and I know I've got to get that right first, so that everything else will follow."

As David began his Skinny Life journey, we discussed the

prevailing truth that he punishes himself to work ever harder and cuts himself no slack. He expressed an intense feeling that he owed it to his family to give them a luxurious lifestyle with nice homes, lavish vacations, and great college educations. In order for David to provide all of this, he felt he could never take a break, never think of himself, or he would be letting down everyone he cared about.

When I asked if he deserved anything for himself, such as time to take care of himself through exercise or healthy eating, he became tearful. He truly felt that he didn't deserve to take time or resources for himself. Over many years, David had developed a complete disregard for himself and his physical health, and he had accepted instead a program of pain and punishment that made him sacrifice all of his energy, time, health, and well-being to make others happy.

I'm happy to say that a window of possibility has been opened to David through the Skinny Life program. This is the hope and the truth he's been waiting for, and he is excited about having the Skinny Life program to support him in making the changes he knows are necessary. When David broke down in front of me, he admitted there would be nothing left of him if he continued the punishing model he'd been living. He was able to admit that if he truly loved God, himself, and his family, he needed to get real and make some very big changes now.

I'm happy to be a part of David's journey and I know his life will be ever more blessed as he learns to honor and love himself and his body. What is the side effect of the program's teaching of self-love and awareness? David has lost eighty pounds so far!

## Avoid Old Fears, Traps, and Diversions

Maybe you recognize yourself in David's story. You might have found, time and again, that something in your life diverted you from focusing on the health and fitness that would add years to your life and give you the quality of life you deserve. It could be excuses about your job, your spouse, your kids, or your schedule. It's time to notice the old fears, traps, diversions, and stories because awareness will help you avoid being tripped up by them again. It gives you the perspective to recognize the old patterns and to say, "No more. I'm absolutely done with this. This is no longer acceptable." Then you can exclaim to yourself and the world, "This is the new me! This person is who I am now!"

## Skinny Life Toolbox

### Change Your Story

As you move forward in your Skinny Life journey and create a new story about yourself, you are going to realize the old story has no power over you anymore, and nothing will give you a greater sense of freedom than letting that old story go! The story David had created his life around was that he belonged to everyone's demands and expectations. But his worst enemy to his body had been his own expectation of serving his job and his family perfectly. David discovered that he wasn't allowing one iota of self-indulgence when it came to taking care of himself and his body. Because his self-sacrificing patterns were so strong, his compensation for that swung just as far in the opposite direction. His only indulgence, break, or pleasure was food, and he had developed an addiction over many years to fatty, sugary, and starch-filled foods that were not good for his body.

Notice what your story is. What do you keep telling yourself over and over that would make it impossible to break the pattern until you identify it? David had to stop saying, "I can't take any time to eat right. I can't take any time to do anything about exercise. My time is not my own." His story changed to, "I have to make these changes or the work I'm doing won't matter. I have to do everything I can to eat healthy foods no matter how hard it seems. I have to get on my bike and pedal no matter what work I have to get done."

**Skinny Life Bottom Line:** As you move forward in your fitness journey and create a new story about yourself, you will realize the old story has no power over you anymore!

## From Feeling Bad to Feeling Good

When interviewing my test group in the beginning of the Skinny Life program, I discovered that for most of them, even when they had engaged in some sort of weight-loss program in the past, they often had taken a self-punishing approach in which they went on a super-rigid, super-low-calorie diet that restricted regular foods and instead substituted some kind of premade concoction as a replacement for meals, for weeks on end. Some had taken controversial injections with promises of special fat-melting hormones, which didn't make a lasting difference in their weight or fitness. The pervasive feeling they described always felt more like pain and punishment than honor and respect.

With Skinny Life you should never feel as if you are putting yourself through pain or punishment. You'll understand that more as we go through chapters 8, 9, and 10, focusing on the new you in eating and movement. For now let's just focus our thoughts on this affirmation. I encourage you to say it out loud:

> I am living my life with the intention of
> taking the very best care of myself.
> I deserve it.

## What Messages Are You Sending Your Cells?

Did you know that every cell in your body is alive and full of intelligent creation? That each cell has inside of it the special codes that make up who you are? The love and intelligence with which our Creator made us is beyond our human comprehension. It is a wonderful feeling when we begin to appreciate how special each cell of our bodies is.

> I am living my life with the intention of taking the very best care of myself. I deserve it.

I want you to imagine right now that your cells are listening to the messages you are sending them. Ask yourself what messages you've been sending these beautiful, perfect cells of yours. If they include any hint of pain, punishment, or self-condemnation, then it's time to change those messages for good.

Even if it sounds funny to send messages to your cells, consider this: If you acknowledge that you've been punishing and inflicting pain on yourself, how much better is it to shine some love and light on even the smallest parts of you?

## Skinny Life Toolbox

### Conquer Weight through Visualization

First, read through this entire visualization exercise and get familiar with it. Then close your eyes in a quiet place and slowly go through it in your mind.

Take three deep breaths and get comfortable and settled into your body. Start to imagine each of the cells that make up your organs, and the organs that make up your systems. See your mind, for now, as the director of that vast number of cells. Now picture the cells as a community, lovingly created and living and working synergistically every day to support you in this life.

As the director and the head of this community of cells, take a moment to be in awe that they can all work together beautifully to provide life and health and all of these intricate functions they do each day, without you even having to worry about it. Feel gratitude for the job your cells do in their innate intelligence, working in harmony together to make each organ function. Shine love upon each of those cells.

Now shine love upon each of your organs, which are groups of cells working together in harmony. See how they function so perfectly for your greatest health.

Now shine loving thanks onto your systems, seeing how the

whole elegant dance of cells, organs, and systems comes together flawlessly.

Now shine love on the whole community that is your body. Imagine your cells, systems, and organs coming together to function better than ever at every level. See them regulating your appetite, see them increasing your metabolic burn, see all of your organs and systems working better than they ever have to create a lean, healthy body for you. Appreciate how beautifully and harmoniously all of this comes together every day, twenty-four hours a day, to support your life and your most healthy presence on this earth.

Give a final thanks to your Creator for the glorious creation of your body. When you're ready, open your eyes.

## First Be, Then Do

Just about every weight-loss program focuses first on how to do: do this and do that, eat this and don't eat that, then you'll be fit. The Skinny Life focuses first on being. Being creates doing. First we *be*, and then we *do*.

Some people say success isn't only something you pursue; success is something you attract by the person you become. Ultimately your actions and habits will spring naturally from who you are and what you truly believe. Anyone can adopt a certain behavior like dieting or exercising for a while, but eventually we will default to the core of who we are inside our subconscious minds. That's why with Skinny Life we dig deeper to build a more connected, caring, authentic relationship with ourselves.

I don't want you to be pressured or intimidated into action.

I want you to become a natural winner at everything in your life, including health and weight mastery. Over time as you live the Skinny Life, your actions and habits will arise from a calm place of knowing exactly who you are and who you want to become, which includes treating yourself with love, honor, and respect in all your choices each day.

**Skinny Life Bottom Line:** As you live the Skinny Life, your actions and habits will arise from a calm place of knowing exactly who you are and who you want to become.

# Affirmations

I am worthy.

I am good enough.

I am lovable.

I deserve the best.

I deserve to be rewarded with the best care for myself.

I am precious to my Creator.

I am precious to the people in my life.

My life is important.

My health is important so that I can live my best life.

# 6

# Releasing My Old Heavy Identity

Whenever we are getting ready to create something new in our lives, we first have to take a very important step. We have to release the old we're not happy with anymore, which then creates the space to have what we want.

In the Skinny Life it's important to examine our identities and what they mean. We need to understand how our identity drives our beliefs, habits, and actions (or lack of actions). Many of us think of our identities as something fixed and unchangeable. But as I've worked with my clients, we've discovered that identities change all the time. In fact, your identity has changed multiple times already during your lifetime. And this is great news!

Think back for a moment about who you were as a three-year-old, how you thought and behaved. As a toddler you probably had very little independence, relying on your parents to guide you and be by your side virtually anytime you were outside the house. You might have only recently learned to potty in a restroom rather than in a diaper. You completely depended on someone to provide you with food at appropriate times of the day, and you were not competent to safely navigate your way in the outside world.

Then think about yourself as a ten-year-old. Were you the same person? Did you have the same sense of self at age three as you did at age ten? You probably knew how to make a simple meal like a peanut butter sandwich, cheese and crackers, or a bowl of cereal. You had developed a sense of dignity and privacy about restroom matters. You probably had your own set of wheels called a bicycle, which could not only take you away from your home and family but allow you to navigate your neighborhood competently by yourself or with friends.

I've never met anyone who had the same sense of self, the same beliefs, the same habits, at age ten as he did at age three. His sense of self changed; the identity he carried as a toddler developed into a completely different identity he exuded as a ten-year-old.

The changing of our very identities happens over and over again as we evolve throughout our lifetimes. You're the same person—but different. You changed identity because you grew physically, mentally, and emotionally. But something else happened to allow you to become that new person, to take on that new identity. In order to do that, you had to *let go* of the old identity.

To become the more independent ten-year-old, you couldn't continue to hang on your mother's shoulder, sucking your thumb and struggling with potty training. You had to let go of your beliefs that you couldn't do things by yourself, that you needed someone by your side every moment. And then as you released those ideas, even though they seemed familiar and brought you a sense of security, you discovered that letting go of that old you allowed for a more mature, better you to come forward. Now the new identity could be born.

And how good it felt to allow the new you to come to life! You felt freer. You felt you could handle things by yourself and that led to a strong sense of power. Letting go of the old identity allowed for a more confident identity to come through as the new you.

## Skinny Life Toolbox

### See Your Negative Identity

Spend a moment right now contemplating the following questions. Without any self-judgment, allow yourself to clearly see whatever negative identity you might be carrying about your health, fitness, and body image.

- Have you accepted the identity that you have weight problems or accepted the belief that you have to fight weight your whole life?
- Have you accepted identifying thoughts that say you aren't able to live a fit, slim, and healthy life, naturally and easily?

I want you to notice your answers because if either of these statements is true, things are about to change for the better.

## False Identity Happens Every Day

Have you ever recalled a memory and thought, *I can't believe I did that!* or *I can't believe I even thought like that!* I've looked back over the decades contemplating a particular state of mind (or a particularly bad hairdo) I had in the past and thought, *That doesn't even seem like me.* And truthfully, it's not you anymore because you are different now from who you were then.

For most people, your identity isn't always what you might think it is. We've all heard stories of children raised in the wild. There was a popular one about a boy who was raised by wolves. Somehow a pack of wolves accepted him as one of them. When years later humans discovered the boy, everything about his behavior, his habits, and his beliefs about himself said *I am a wolf.* His very identity had been molded to become that of a wolf. We know that this boy was a human being. But because of his environment, he had developed a false identity.

I know this seems extreme, but people develop false identities all the time. In the case of weight issues, many people have absorbed beliefs that made them think they were *destined* to be heavy and to have weight problems. Somewhere along the line, conditioning, experiences, and the people around them said they would always need to fear becoming overweight.

What many of my clients discover in our work together is that, just like the boy who thought he was a wolf, they had taken on identities that weren't true. These men and women were not doomed to weight issues. They were not preprogrammed to be fat people. They had simply picked up the wrong cues from their environments.

This discovery was magical to them! As they began to let go of those false identities, they realized they were something different. Just like the three-year-old who eventually became the ten-year-old, the person with chronic weight issues became the person who was destined to become naturally fit and slim.

All they had to do was to let go of the false identity and to change their environment—and that part became easy because they had a Skinny Life lifestyle, which provided the new environment. As they let go of the old identity and kept reinforcing the new thought patterns, they learned to integrate the Skinny Life into every part of their lives. They started immersing themselves in their new identities and the naturally fit, slim, healthy people they were always meant to be.

> When you realize that the identity you've taken on isn't necessarily the real you, it opens so many doors in your life.

When you realize that the identity you've taken on isn't necessarily the real you, it opens so many doors in your life. The identities we adopt are really nothing more than stories about ourselves that we've allowed to be written into our subconscious minds. These stories contain pieces of interactions and experiences that we hold on to, even though holding on to them isn't serving us and keeps us stuck in an unwanted identity.

These stories contain other concepts about our body shape and size and the many fears we weave into those identities, such as feeling out of control or not being good enough or lovable. Without knowing it, we hold on to those stories even though they are false and full of negative emotions and limiting beliefs.

## Skinny Life Toolbox

### Break Down Old Walls

Here is a great mind tool that will help release the old, negative parts of your identity and start to rebuild the new you: naturally fit, slim, healthy, and loving life! Read through this entire exercise once, and then enact it in your imagination to reinforce its effect.

Imagine for a moment that in the past, you were so certain that you would always struggle with weight that you erected a wall around that identity and thought the wall served a purpose. Maybe the wall gave you a false sense of protection or security from hurt or pain or the fear of gaining weight. Maybe it didn't allow others to see your pain or even to see the real you. The reasons we erect such psychological barriers don't matter because once we recognize them, or become aware of them, we can bring them down.

Even if you don't think you've erected a barrier, I want you to imagine that you become aware of a wall you put up around an old weight identity and that you can actually see it. As you gaze at this wall, seeing it and feeling it around you, notice fully the limitations the wall has put on you: how stifling and unbearable it feels and how it chokes off your freedom to have the health and fitness that are part of who you really are. Imagine feeling the confinement of this wall intensely but then realizing the wall is not built on strength or truth. It appears impenetrable, but in reality it is actually a very weak wall, and you see its fragility now. It almost seems ridiculous that the wall was ever there!

You decide you don't want that wall confining you anymore, so you simply reach out and push down the wall. You're amazed at how easily it falls; even though it appeared to be sturdy, it was poorly built. See the wall crumble around you, and see yourself stepping out from the confines of that wall. You instantly feel everything that doesn't support your greatest fitness and health also crumble, disintegrating into dust. Now you step through and walk forward, feeling rays of light shining down, permeating your body, making you feel new and alive.

Walking away from the old, imagine you see a circle of excellence in front of you. If you're ready to keep moving forward, make the decision to step into that circle. You notice as you enter the circle that you are in the company of other people like yourself who live in conscious awareness about their health and fitness. Just as these people understand how to integrate health, fitness, and a love for movement into their lives, you also understand that you can integrate and live the Skinny Life.

Read through this exercise several times and bookmark it to come back to when you need it. Know that if you ever have a weak moment or a tough day as you're living your new Skinny Life, you can simply close your eyes for a moment and envision stepping into this circle of excellence. And when you take a breath from that new mind space, instantly see and feel those rays of light filling you, energizing you, and anchoring you to the new fit, slim version of you.

## Craft a New Blueprint

You'll begin to notice the benefits of these exercises in other areas of your life. Because you are a whole person, when you begin to improve one area of your life, such as your health and fitness, you will find that other areas, such as relationships or your career, start to improve. Your thoughts, emotions, physical body, and spiritual presence for God are all woven together into this elegant symphony every moment of your life. When one area suffers, the whole you suffers. When one area begins to heal and shine, so do the other areas.

As you use the Skinny Life Toolboxes and absorb insight from this reading journey, you'll start to feel much better about yourself right away. That's because God programmed you for excellence in all areas of your life, including your health and fitness. The real you, the best you is always waiting inside to be released. Life is about continually evolving, becoming the next best version of you, and just as the three-year-old takes on a new identity as the ten-year-old, you will be able to take on a brand-new, fit, slim identity as you release the old you forever.

 **Skinny Life Bottom Line:** The real you, the best you is always waiting inside to be released.

When we accept beliefs about ourselves, we allow those beliefs to create the blueprint of what we become. It's time to be done with the old beliefs and thought programs that supported your old identity and to deliberately create new programs that support your greatest health, shape, and fitness. Remember, changing old thought and belief patterns requires dedication and repetition. As you break down those old patterns and implement new ones, you will easily and effortlessly live the Skinny Life and love it!

# Affirmations

I can clearly see that I had thought patterns that became belief patterns, and that some of those beliefs don't support my greatest health and fitness.

I can clearly see how I developed a false identity about my weight and fitness from those flawed beliefs.

I can now happily release those old beliefs and thought patterns that kept me stuck in a negative mind-set and body that was less than my true self.

I am willing now to release the old heavy identity and to embrace a new healthy, fit identity.

My old weight issue identity is a thing of the past.

I *love* my new slim identity. I *love* the brand-new me.

# 7

# Building My Healthy New Identity

I love to think of our days on earth as a journey of transformation. The Skinny Life journey is much the same. As we discussed in the previous chapter, you have to let go of the old identity and break down the negative self-image related to weight issues before you can move forward into consciously creating the new you and accepting your new identity as a healthy, fit person.

I like to call this *clean slate time*. It's time to get a new vision of you and to see it already set in motion. We have acknowledged that your negative thoughts about yourself were there because you allowed them in. But now you know you don't have to allow those thoughts anymore!

The next skill I'd like to teach you is one of the most important. It will help you experience success not only in your Skinny Life journey, but also in every area of your life. This important tool of transformation is the skill of observation. As you develop greater ability to observe you will see the truth in each situation, especially in your health and wellness, and you will know exactly how to act on it.

Observation is an essential step toward lasting change. To change something, you must first be able to discern the way it is now. Observation allows us to step out of our routine ways of seeing and thinking. Truly observing something lets you set yourself apart from it and look at it objectively.

## Observe Your Thoughts

The first area in which we must become proficient in the art of observation is in our thoughts. Often people become confused and begin to think their thoughts are all *true*. When you observe your thoughts, you learn to deliberately and effectively use your mind so your mind doesn't use you! Pausing to become an observer of your own perceptions will put you at the gateway of profound life change. The observation process is the catalyst for learning to separate yourself from what is running through your mind.

## Skinny Life Toolbox

### Thought Observation Exercise

Close your eyes, take a few deep breaths, and clear your mind. If a thought pops into your mind, observe it in a detached way, as if it is a leaf drifting past you in the wind. You're aware of it blowing by, but it is not connected to you at all. Make sure you are observing your thoughts as they go by, but don't judge or respond to them in any way. Just notice them. Continue this exercise for a few minutes.

After you have done this for a couple of minutes, keeping your eyes closed, ask, *Who is observing these thoughts that drift through my mind?* Then listen for the answer, which is of course, *I am.* When you feel ready, open your eyes. It's important to ask that question each time and let yourself feel the answer as it comes from you.

This is the part of you I like to call the *Observer.* The Observer in you realizes the separateness between you and your thoughts. Your Observer is the part of you that is in tune with that still, small voice, the part of you that knows when God is trying to get your attention.

> People's minds are changed through observation and not through argument.
> —Will Rogers

The Observer can objectively notice the quality and content of what you are feeling, saying, or doing. We've all had moments when we've said, *I'm surprised I just said that,* or *I really don't know why I'm doing this.* Once you tap into this wonderful Observer part of you and begin to understand the separation between you and your thoughts, then you can make more deliberate, positive choices on behalf of your health, fitness, and emotional well-being. You will also understand that the thoughts, perceptions, and beliefs you've formed don't necessarily have to be there. Even though those thought patterns felt like you, or who you were before, now you understand they are just thoughts. Thoughts can be changed once you are aware of them.

## Skinny Lifers Share Key Observations

Here are some key observations that have made some Skinny Lifers' journeys a lot easier.

Cheryl said:

If I went off track and ate something I didn't feel good about, like a candy bar, I observed that I would tell myself that I've already blown it, so I might as well just blow it the rest of the day. That way of thinking would cause me to take one small indulgence that I could overcome with a good strong walk and turn it into an excuse to dive into doughnuts, ice cream, and other unhealthy foods that day. Then I'd be back on a bingeing streak.

Now when I indulge, I observe that old voice and turn it into a new voice that tells me I've had a treat today, so I'll make up for it by balancing out my eating with a big salad and some protein for dinner and a jog after work. It feels so good to "catch" myself through observation and not take a headlong dive into self-sabotaging behaviors.

Christina told me:

Through all of the up-and-down dieting I had done in my life, I continued to tell myself that I didn't have time to do the things it took to eat healthy. I was too busy. People just didn't understand. When I finally saw the simplicity of the Skinny Life and just made sure once a week I went to the grocery store to get healthy foods, it made it so much easier!

I started using my Observer a lot more regularly. When I found myself reaching for something bad, my Observer started to catch the lie sneaking up. Whenever I would start to think I was too busy to eat right, suddenly from my Observer perspective I would catch that thought and say, *You have all the healthy food you need. There's no need to hinder the great progress you're making. Grab some healthy snacks from the pantry.* I started to realize that my former excuses were just that. There are usually plenty of healthy options around or nearby.

## Meet Vivienne

One of my dear clients, Vivienne, joined the Skinny Life program after thirty diets had left her heavier each time. With a zero success rate, she was truly at a loss. She had been afraid of food and of her body for as long as she could remember. To her, mealtimes were opportunities to feel guilty and anxious rather than a time to nourish and enjoy.

After Vivienne began applying the principles and techniques in the Skinny Life program, she shared her excitement that she was becoming more honest and aware about her relationship with food and with herself. Her ability to do that came from learning to observe what was going on in her mind without judging it or herself. Here's what she said:

I became much more aware of what I was telling myself every day. It was very eye-opening and made me more observant. The Skinny Life has made such a positive difference in my moods. Now that I know when I'm being hard on myself I can make changes. I've become a lot nicer to myself, not beating myself up as much. It has been amazing! My outlook and the way I treated myself started to change. When you do that, your body ends up losing the weight and you don't even have to work hard at it. First it's conscious, then it's subconscious. It comes to the point where it's just your lifestyle. You end up dropping the weight because that's how you live.

Vivienne's story is an example of how our worst fears often create what we are getting in life. Constant worry and fear are like subtle prayers you're sending out—but you're asking for what you don't want. Vivienne began by valuing the gift of her body, which eased her anxiety about her body image and food and allowed her to give herself a higher, more conscious quality of care. Eating healthy and doing fun activities and exercise became joyful and easy because they sprang from a place of love and self-honoring rather than self-condemnation.

## Dare to Dream

I believe God gifted us with our own imaginations to lift his work of creation (us) to even higher levels. We are God's own masterpieces, but we are masterpieces in the making. That's why he gave us the power to choose. He didn't preprogram us to make the right decisions, to honor the stunning creation of our bodies. Instead he loved us enough to give us free will to make our decisions and create from our own imaginations what we will become, how we will live our lives, and how we will treat ourselves.

God invites us to imagine ourselves as the very best we can be, caring for our bodies and becoming fully healthy and whole. But the free will he gifted us with also gives us the opportunity to imagine ourselves as less than our best. When those dark, self-defeating thoughts cloud our awareness, no matter how subtle they are, they drive us away from our best life and leave us feeling far from God's glory and splendor. Everything in and about God is pure, clean, and whole. To live a happy and satisfying life, our bodies must be a reflection of that purity, cleanliness, and wholeness in the way we think, move, eat, and care for ourselves. Now is the time to experience that beautiful reality.

## Begin Crafting Your Best You

We're ready now for the act of *conscious creating*. We start by asking, who am I? This time your goal is to answer this question, not with the negative perceptions of your past, but with the voice that you have begun to observe within. As we have seen, deep inside you is a place where you can hear your own pure, clear voice guided by your Creator, free from anyone else's baggage or opinion. When you ask, who am I? from this place of observation, you will get a brand-new answer.

When you do this, you will discover you are much more than you ever thought you were. You start to see glimpses of the person God created you to be at your best. Any of us can reach that place when we have cleared away our old thoughts and beliefs. There you will realize that you are far, far more than you ever imagined. As you fill yourself with God's presence you will realize you are capable of achieving your dreams and becoming the healthy, whole person you were meant to be. You will realize you are capable of living a masterful life in your health, fitness, and every other area.

Life will always have its ups and downs. We all feel a little puny at times and at other times we feel powerful. What we want to do is learn and embrace tools and techniques that allow us to get through rough waters without hurting our health and failing ourselves. One of my favorite quick fixes is to spend a few moments in silence reminding myself that I don't have to do anything alone in life. That it's really an illusion when I'm feeling puny, alone, or out of options. I simply find a few minutes in a quiet space, breathe deeply several times, and say, "God, without you I'm nothing, but with you I'm everything. Fill me with you."

This simple prayer exercise always gives me a sense of calm, renewed energy. It's easy to get dragged down in life and forget who you are. You were designed by the Master Creator. When you are distraught, broken, or in a self-destructive mode, you have just temporarily lost touch with that design.

It is so exciting when you discover the power in envisioning and consciously creating the new you! All of us have let a lot of other forces—media, our upbringing, circumstances, negative experiences—contribute to who we've become. It's thrilling to know that you can now create who you want to be deliberately, consciously, and truthfully under God's guiding hand.

When you begin asking and answering the question, who am I? be patient with yourself. Remember, this is just the beginning. As you continue to progress through the Skinny Life, your answers will become more certain and more powerful.

## Define Yourself Differently

As you deliberately practice filling yourself with God's presence you'll start to feel and see a new you emerging. You will define yourself differently. You will develop a new self-identity that is whole and complete and not lacking in anything.

Here are some great examples of clients who began to define themselves differently.

Camille came to me saying, "I'm someone who has always looked at food and gained weight." That changed to, "I'm a woman whose body responds to the loving care I give it. I'm aware of the best ways to love my body and care for it."

Gina came to me saying, "I come from a family of heavy people. I'm a fat person because fat genes run in my family." That changed to, "My genes are activated by my environment. I'm a person who creates the ideal environment for my genes to express my best health."

Suzanne came to me saying, "I'm a binge eater. When I'm stressed and upset, food is the only thing that soothes me." That changed to, "Food isn't my master. I'm a master at choosing the right foods for the right reasons. I eat for my greatest health."

The way we define ourselves matters. As you move through the Skinny Life process you will find a new and empowering answer to the question, who am I?

**Skinny Life Bottom Line:** You can now create who you want to be more deliberately, consciously, and truthfully under God's guiding hand.

# Skinny Life Toolbox

## Let's Begin the Creation Process!

Make sure that you're making time for yourself to do this conscious creation deliberately and without distraction. It's important to set aside quiet, prayerful reflection and meditation time for the creation process.

I want you to say out loud three times: "My self-image is nothing more than how I see myself in my own imagination."

You're going to begin projecting your new image to the world *now*, so we need to be clear about what that image is. Following are some powerful questions. Answer these from the perspective of being in the best shape of your life and feeling totally comfortable and energized by it. If it's difficult for you to remember a time you felt that way, then I'm going to ask you to suspend all disbelief and imagine it. Make sure you're tracking the questions and answers in a journal.

- How will life be different when you get really fit and slim, and it feels easy for you?
- In that healthy state, what will you be doing with yourself? What are some new things you'll be doing with your time?
- What will your new resources be? How will you utilize those resources for your maximum benefit?
- How do you want to feel then? How will that compare to how you felt before?

- What feelings, thoughts, and habits will you be free of forever?
- How will you treat yourself differently from the way you have in the past?

Read the answers to these questions out loud, as often as you can, in the first few months of your Skinny Life journey.

Remember, as you project your new image to the world, not only will the world respond to it, but you will find yourself becoming that person. You are generating a brand-new you and only you are in charge of that! You are the gatekeeper, and only you get to decide who you really are and who you are becoming.

The answers to these important questions will begin to build the new story and ultimately *become* the new you! The questions will create a much deeper awareness about yourself—to honor where you are now, to know you are growing and evolving in stages, and to understand that each stage will be more beautiful than the next, bringing you to a new place of freedom each time.

Some people feel a bit overwhelmed at this point, thinking they have to have all of the answers and progress at once. But the Skinny Life is not an end; it is a process. It is a lifestyle. It is a new you with new beginnings every day. It is about being conscious of everything about you.

 **Skinny Life Bottom Line:** The Skinny Life is not an end, it is a process. It is a lifestyle.

## There Are No Limits

There are no limits to your greatest health and fitness. Each day I want you to look forward to saying hello to a new, fit, slim you. Each day, I want you to celebrate your body and your life!

In Skinny Life we're tearing down the old mental structure that brought out the unwanted in your life, and we're rebuilding the mental structure that supports what you do want. You are already experiencing success. Keep going!

# Affirmations

I am starting with a clean slate.

I am creating a new vision of myself.

I am a skillful observer of my thoughts.

I am separate from my thoughts.

I observe when I have self-sabotaging thoughts
that don't serve me.

I am a masterpiece in the making.

I am redefining who I am.

# Part Three

# Life As the New You

# 8

# The New Me: My Mind

Welcome to a new you. I mean that! So far in this book we have spent a fair amount of time understanding and unwinding the negative patterns and beliefs that worked against you in your health, fitness, and wholeness. God's most beautiful manifestation of you will never spring from that dark, self-defeating place of the past, so we've decided to pull the plug on it forever.

From this point forward in the book we will get into a new mind-set that is all about how you are thinking, feeling, eating, and moving as *the new you*. It may seem strange to you at times, because we are going to talk and act as if the new you has already happened or is happening. This is a key strategy for success. As you act on what you hope for, you begin to live as the new person you have been imagining. What will gradually come to exist is the new, happy, fit, slim you!

We'll embrace this new identity in three areas: our minds, the foods we eat, and the movements we make.

**Mind**: The new you is conscious of your thoughts and emotions. You'll realize what they mean and what they are trying to teach you.

**Eat**: The new you is conscious of the foods you're putting into your magnificent body and how each food helps make or keep you fit. You'll consider each food before you eat it: will it add to your energy, health, and fitness or put a burden on your health, strength, and well-being?

**Move**: The new you will be tuned in to your body's need to move, to sway, to jump, to run, and to stretch. You will begin to see the person you imagined: someone who is in touch with those needs and uses movement as a part of your everyday life and support system.

We'll tackle these areas in the pages ahead, beginning with the mind.

## Take Charge of Your Life

Let's talk about an arrow in your new Skinny Life quiver that will help you hit the mark every time in achieving what you desire. That straight and pointed arrow is the virtue of *responsibility*, which of course we use via our minds. Why do so many people have difficulty accepting responsibility for what they are getting in their lives? People who shift blame and shirk responsibility somehow feel they're exonerated from the negative outcome they're experiencing. This is a form of self-deception because the truth is this: No one owns the outcome of your life except you. Period. Taking full responsibility for your life, your health, and your wellness requires both guts and decisive action, and this can sometimes feel demanding to those who have historically run away from it.

 **Skinny Life Bottom Line:** No one owns the outcome of your life except you. Period.

But when you take the responsibility for your health and wellness, you take up the power and authority over your life that God meant for you alone. These are sacred gifts. In your new mindset, the key to claiming this ownership is learning to rely on your internal resources. If you don't do this, then outside events, conditions, or voices could cause you to decide it's just too difficult to eat delicious, wholesome foods, or to find ways to weave healthy movement into your life. But the new you *never* lets those things undermine your clear decision to honor your body.

The new you owns herself and her choices. No making excuses or blaming others. We'll talk more in the following chapters about specific solutions that make it easy and natural to choose on behalf of your best self in eating and movement every time. *That* is the new you in your mind that we're talking about! The new you accepts full responsibility for creating and sustaining your greatest health, fitness, and wholeness.

## Set Boundaries

A part of taking responsibility is activating boundaries around your commitment to your health and fitness. Often even the people we love will draw on our time, energy, and resources incessantly until there's nothing left. Self-care goes down the drain.

It's important to write out a reasonable plan for how you will fit in healthy movement and eating every day, including the most convenient, reasonable, and economically feasible ways to carry out your plan. We've talked in previous chapters about how there are times when you have to put your needs above those of others. One of those times is when your health and wholeness are suffering. It's very difficult to give to others when your own cup is empty. When your cup is overflowing with energy from self-honoring, then you will have a lot more to offer to others.

If you haven't already, decide now to be your own advocate. If you are waiting for someone else to do it, you might wait forever. Looking out for yourself and your own needs not only fosters appropriate respect from the people who love you, but it often will inspire them to do the same for themselves. I've seen an entire family dynamic changed for the better when Mom or Dad decided to embrace the Skinny Life. It's especially good when spouses, siblings, or friends come together to live a more dynamic, fun lifestyle of honoring and caring for themselves.

## Clear Out the Vampires

A powerful inner and outer renewal is occurring as you begin to practice the Skinny Life. You can take your life to the next level of vibrant, dynamic health, energy, and fitness by *clutter clearing*. It's difficult to bring exciting new experiences into your life when your personal space—including the time and energy spent in relationships—is full of unnecessary stuff.

Clutter clearing includes getting rid of all of the junk that slows you down or makes you feel chaotic. Sometimes, letting go of destructive relationships is part of the clutter-clearing process. You've heard the term *emotional vampires*? These are people who suck the life out of you by pouring out their problems on you and expecting you to make them yours. We want to be supportive of people, especially those close to us, but we have to watch out for those who drain our energy without giving back. As long as we allow emotional vampires in our space, they will devour it, leaving us frustrated that these interactions waste valuable time and energy. Remember, everyone is responsible for his or her own happiness and health—just as you are.

> Emotional vampires are the people who suck the life out of you by pouring out their problems on you and expecting you to make them yours.

Emotional vampires can be destructive in several ways. Often they criticize you for making good new choices on your own behalf. Usually this derives from feelings of jealousy. They'll subtly condemn you and try to make you feel guilty or selfish. These are the people for whom you need to erect the most definite boundaries. Sometimes the people we love the most are the ones who need our firmest boundaries. Save your time and energy for engaging in activities that keep you fit, active, and healthy! Let the vampires take care of themselves.

Lynn, a client, had become close to a friend, Ruth, she'd met when she moved to her new town. As Lynn began to absorb the Skinny Life philosophies, she started to realize her relationship with

Ruth was based entirely on eating. Their primary source of entertainment was going to giant all-you-can-eat buffets and laughing about how much they loved the pastas and desserts. When Lynn approached her friend about the positive changes she wanted to implement in her life, Ruth laughed it off and continually tried to pull her off track.

So Lynn tried setting boundaries. She asked kindly in a number of ways for Ruth's support in her weight-loss journey:

- She gave a heartfelt admission that she didn't feel good about the overeating they were indulging in.
- She asked Ruth to help her pick other activities they would enjoy together such as walking, hiking, or riding bikes.
- She gave her a schedule of times she would be doing healthy exercise or outdoor activities, no matter what, and invited her to join in if she liked.
- She shared a list of the wonderful foods that she was committed to eating now and the foods she would no longer put in her precious body, and she asked for Ruth's support in sticking with her commitment.
- Instead of going to buffets where they overate, she invited Ruth to have fun in the kitchen creating delicious recipes using lots of vegetables, lean healthy meats, and whole grains and fruit. It would save money and prevent them from indulging in cheesy pastas, fried foods, and mountains of desserts.
- She asked Ruth to take her desire to be healthy seriously because, all kidding aside, Lynn was really getting

concerned about her health with the extra weight she was carrying.

Ruth continued to dismiss Lynn's pleas to support her in these changes and continued to tempt her into huge buffets and double fudge brownie sundaes, saying things like, "Oh, lighten up. We should celebrate that your son got an A on his test." She would regularly come up with reasons to "celebrate" or "reward" themselves after a hard day. She would also often come over during Lynn's planned workout time to tell her about another problem she was having and distract Lynn from her exercise.

Eventually, after Lynn realized Ruth wasn't going to stop joking about or making fun of her efforts, Lynn decided that this relationship wouldn't be long lived. Despite repeated requests, Ruth refused to support Lynn's desire and commitment to take care of her body and health. Again, this kind of emotional vampire doesn't respect boundaries—so he or she has to be unincluded from your life activities.

The more deliberately you decide to continue the Skinny Life journey, the more you will build your resolve, your personal power, and your new sense of self. You'll notice in your attitudes, your weight, your fitness, and even your everyday life that your new identity is so much more powerful than the old one! The Skinny Life teaches that nothing is impossible, including decluttering your life and mind.

 **Skinny Life Bottom Line:** Your new identity is so much more powerful than the old one!

## Skinny Life Toolbox

### Positive Feelings Anchoring Exercise

Did you know that you carry the means to collapse painful feelings? I'm going to teach you a technique right now.

I like to have you involve your body in some mind exercises, because studies now show that memories are stored not only in the brain, but in a connected network throughout the body. The groundbreaking work featured in Dr. Candace Pert's book *Molecules of Emotion: The Science behind Mind-Body Medicine* teaches that when we keep repeating thoughts or exist in a certain emotional state much of the time, our brains and bodies store this chemistry and its corresponding cell behaviors, which become learned patterns in our minds and bodies. Brain cells aren't the only ones that have the ability to hold memory. Cells throughout the body have memory capability. Memories are constantly being transmitted through bundles of nerve cells that run all the way down the spinal cord and out into the organs, even reaching the skin's surface.[1] When we're restructuring our thought-emotion patterns, it's important to involve our physical body because our body has been involved in the storage of these memories. You'll see how we do that in this exercise.

This exercise will help you purge negative feelings and then anchor positive feelings and the vision of the brand-new you.

Sit somewhere you can close your eyes for a few minutes. First, while squeezing your right knee with your right hand, I want you to think back to an experience when you felt really great inside. Tap into this experience of feeling safe, centered, peaceful, confident, or courageous. Think about an actual event that made you feel these desired, positive emotions, perhaps when you received a compliment or an award. Allow yourself to really feel those positive emotions. While continuing to think of the experience, release your knee, open your eyes, and take a deep breath.

Next, squeeze your left knee with your left hand as you think about an experience when you were dissatisfied with the way you behaved or performed. Allow yourself to experience the negative emotion. While still feeling those emotions, release your left knee, open your eyes, and take a deep breath.

Now I want you to think of your preferred response to a negative situation by tapping into your inner resources. If you felt out of control in that negative event, what qualities and feelings would have made you feel more in control? Perhaps it's the feeling you've had when someone really needed your talent or help on something. Maybe it's just the feeling of lying on the beach in total relaxation. Pick something that counteracts those negative feelings.

Again, with your right hand squeezing your right knee, anchor those positive feelings and resources on top of the other good feelings. Now, holding those thoughts and feeling the security of those inner resources, squeeze both knees for about sixty seconds, collapsing all of the negative feelings into the positive and noticing the positive feelings taking over. Notice the feelings of strength and calmness as you turn over any negativity to these inner resources.

You have resources of positive strength that can be another tool in overcoming any form of negativity. You're deliberately drawing on positive experiences rather than negative experiences and getting in touch with those memories that are stored in your physical body. Just allow them to work for you. Now let go of both knees, open your eyes, and take a big, cleansing breath.

Use this technique whenever any negative or sabotaging thoughts come up. When you learn to notice your emotional reactions, then learn to deliberately manage them, you take yourself in a new direction that leads to a total transformation of your thought patterns, habits, and ultimately your body. (I suggest you look at www.skinnylife.com, because on that website we will keep adding new techniques to assist in your weight mastery journey.)

## New Thoughts = New Mind

The idea is to increase the frequency of thoughts that make you feel powerful and capable in your own life. Eventually you will replace the old, negative recordings with new, positive ones. You will begin to feel naturally strong . . . trusting and loving yourself. Your mind will have a different belief structure about who you are and what you are capable of.

# Affirmations

I am free to create anything I want in my life.

Only I can decide who I want to be emotionally,
mentally, and physically.

I am deciding to free myself of all limitations.

I will not impose limitations on myself.

I will not allow others to impose limitations on me.

The essence of who I am is completely independent
of my surroundings.

I create who I am no matter what surrounds me.

I have the power to choose. I choose who I am
in any given moment.

I am discovering my own excellence.

I am living an excellent life.

I am expressing and experiencing excellence.

Moment by moment I choose excellent health and fitness.

I love being the new me.

I love being an expert in my own health and fitness.

I love living the fit, healthy Skinny Life!

# 9

# The New Me: My Eating

The Skinny Life is designed to be a comprehensive approach to weight issues encompassing the three important components—Mind, Eat, Move—so we don't leave out any important piece of our health and fitness puzzle. We started with our minds in the previous chapter. Now we're moving into the proper understanding of eating and food.

Overeating is a sensitive, puzzling, and much-discussed topic. Many people wonder what causes them to eat the way they do, and they don't seem to know how to stop!

As a child did you hear, as I did, that you should clean your plate because "there are starving people out there"? Yet according to a report updated in 2015 by the World Health Organization (WHO), more people are dying today from being overweight than from being underweight. WHO found that most of the world's population lives in countries where overweight and obesity kills more people than malnutrition.[1] This is partly due to the majority of people having access to *too much food*, and partly due to the fact that the foods they have access to are processed and sugar laden, which destroy health.

## Mom's Giant Gardens

Growing up in a family of eleven in a small town in Idaho, I learned at a very young age the foundations of living, eating, and moving naturally to create a lifetime of optimal health and fitness. Eating organically, working and playing in the fresh air and sunshine, and discovering the body's natural ability to heal and stay fit were part of my daily rearing.

Looking back, I think it was a rather old-fashioned way of living. Both of my parents had been raised in rural areas with farming and big gardens. Each summer day in Idaho, while my friends raced out the door to find other kids to play with, I was expected to work in my mother's garden before I had free time. This was not a tiny backyard garden—it took up half of a huge pasture area on the three acres behind our house.

I spent many of my summer hours planting, weeding, hoeing, picking, snapping, snipping, and during the last month, stuffing. (That's the time when all of those freshly grown organic fruits and vegetables were stuffed into big shiny Mason jars and canned at the peak of freshness to be eaten all year.) Many days our entire meals were arrays of fresh vegetables: corn on the cob, sliced tomatoes, sautéed zucchini, and mixed lettuces and radishes with olive oil and vinegar.

While other kids were munching on cookies and drinking sodas, our snacks were well water, fruits and veggies, and stone-ground-grain bread and crackers. My mother served her famous chocolate cake only on birthdays.

At the time I thought I had it tough. Now I'm grateful for my mother, who studied natural health and worked to pass that legacy on to me. We ate organic and did juice cleanses long before they became chic, as they are in our pop culture today. My mother also bought non-GMO (genetically modified organism) organic wheat and ground it into flour for bread way ahead of the political GMO outcry that's happening now.[2]

Here's the truly amazing thing. We rarely went to the doctor and almost never took any medicines (including antibiotics). Mom treated the occasional colds we caught with freshly squeezed warm lemonade with honey, vegetable or chicken soups, and a day or two resting in bed. Was the exceptional health of nine children just good luck or good genes? I don't think so, because when we left home, the siblings who deviated from our family traditions seemed to develop more health challenges.

The principles that were ingrained in me from my youth have resulted in my living an extraordinarily healthy life. And they are what inspires me to educate as many people as I can to discover their bodies' own ability to have health and fitness.

## You and Food: A New Relationship

The Skinny Life—the new you in your eating—starts with understanding that you have a relationship with food. It's either a healthy relationship or an unhealthy one. Just as you would in a relationship with a beloved, I want you to learn to know food better. I want you to understand what the food you put into your body is all about.

What properties make up the products you are eating? I want you to know the qualities and benefits of what you eat, and just as you evaluate whether a relationship enhances your life or not, I want you to discern which foods really serve your body and which don't.

You wouldn't invite someone into your home to live with you without knowing if he or she brings value to your life. In Skinny Life we look at food with the same level of conscious awareness. When you look at a cantaloupe, an apple, fresh garden greens, or a high-quality source of protein, what you'll find beneath the surface are things constructed by nature, loaded with vitamin complexes, proteins, enzymes, minerals, and phytochemicals—bioactive compounds that positively affect health. God designed these foods to enter your body and synergistically work with your cells to create health, healing, and energy.

If you were courting someone and found out she had an unhealthy past or disruptive patterns that could create serious problems for you—patterns that could negatively impact your health and even cause premature death—would you start a lifelong relationship with her? Of course not. But it's a great metaphor for most people's relationships with food, especially folks who struggle with their weight, fitness, and health. You have let the wrong foods in. Just as in a codependent relationship, you have continued to do it without truly understanding the devastating effect those foods are having on your health and longevity.

Just as someone who loves you would intervene if he saw you going down the courtship trail with a toxic person, it's time for the new you to intervene from a place of self-love and self-honoring. It's time to embrace a new paradigm in your relationship with food.

The new you has the awareness, understanding, and resolve to know the quality of everything that is going into your body. The new you has a whole new commitment to excellence when it comes to the care of the number-one person God put you in charge of—you.

 **Skinny Life Bottom Line:** The new you has a whole new commitment to excellence when it comes to the care of the number-one person God put you in charge of—you.

## What Doesn't Work

Diets don't work. In fact, they can promote weight gain,[3] increase your chances of being overweight,[4] generate binge eating, and inspire a preoccupation with food.[5]

Why isn't dieting effective? Because it fights your own biology. Restricting food consumption, especially without focusing on the quality of the food involved, gives specific instructions to your body to store fat because it thinks it's in starvation mode. Your body is very intelligent and wired for survival. Over time, dieting changes your set point, which is the level at which your body seeks to maintain itself. It's what most people think of as their metabolism. If you have a low metabolism, you have a high set point. If you have a high metabolism, you have a low set point at which your body says, "Okay, we're at the mark—time to kick up the metabolic burn."

People sabotage their set points through chronic dieting and eating poor-quality food. Genes play a role in determining our body types, but studies have proven that the way you eat is the biggest factor in determining if you will be heavy or slim.[6]

We've also determined that counting calories is counter-productive to weight loss (see chapter 3). When you rely on counting calories, you are focusing on *food calorie quantity*, not on *food quality*. For decades, counting calories was the universal standard for weight loss. It seemed logical: eat this many calories and then do this much exercise or activity to burn it off. Yet science is showing us that the calorie-counting philosophy is wrong, wrong, wrong. A calorie count is a very unreliable determiner of how your body will process and metabolize food, and how lean or fat you will become from eating that food.

> A calorie count is a very unreliable determiner of how lean or fat you will become from eating.

For example: A frosted doughnut contains about 268 calories. A four-ounce chicken breast with two cups of salad with mixed veggies plus one tablespoon of olive oil has about 265 calories. You have a choice between two different foods with about the same calories. That's where the similarity ends. The minute either one of these choices enters your body, you will set off a cascade of metabolic events.

If you choose the doughnut, then the rush of sugar (refined white flour turns quickly to sugar in the body) will alert your pancreas to a sugar overload. In other words, your body is getting too much sugar too fast. That leads to hormonal chaos in your body.

If instead you eat the chicken and salad, then you will cause a much stronger thermic effect in your body, meaning that your body has to burn more energy (calories) to digest and process that food. High-quality proteins burn 20 to 35 percent of the total calories to process the food. In addition, vegetables like spinach increase the feeling of fullness and decrease hunger due to their high water content and high fiber content. The water and fiber add weight and bulk without adding calories, and the fiber slows emptying of the gastric tract, decreasing hunger. Both of these factors contribute to the satiating effect of vegetables and fruits. Not only that, the high quality nourishment you're getting with the chicken and spinach versus the lack of real nutrition from the doughnut is a huge factor in a creating healthy, satisfied body.[7]

You can see how useless calorie counting is when you can have the same calorie count but a vastly better effect in your body depending on the food source. Yet the calorie-counting mind-set is so entrenched in our culture that Skinny Lifers often have to remind themselves to stop!

Dr. Wayne Miller published a clinical study in the *Journal of the Academy of Nutrition and Dietetics* on the relationship between calories and body fat. It turns out there was no relationship! In the study, with all calories being equal, the only thing that led to being overweight was the ratio of sugars/fats versus proteins/healthy, fiber-filled carbohydrates that participants consumed. Dr. Miller concluded that eating simple sugars and refined starches triggers fat-storing hormones and a fat body. Eating healthy proteins and fiber-filled carbohydrates found in vegetables creates a lean body.[8]

A later study published in *Diabetologia* compared high-fat and high-protein diets against a high-carbohydrate diet in insulin-resistant obese women. Body weight, waist circumference, triglycerides, and insulin levels decreased with all three diets. But apart from insulin, the reductions were significantly greater in the high-fat and high-protein groups than in the high-carbohydrate group.[9]

Other studies showed convincing evidence that a higher protein intake increases thermogenesis and satiety compared to diets of lower protein content. The study also showed that lean protein meals lead to reduced calorie intake later, because the subject felt more satisfied longer, and have a lowering effect on blood pressure.[10]

The Skinny Life way of eating stresses quality over calorie counting. I like to think of each food as being coded to do specific things in your body: high-quality foods have a high-quality effect, while poor-quality foods have a negative or low-quality effect. Try to see yourself as a gourmet eater, eating and enjoying only the finest quality of foods and simply passing on the rest.

## THIEF Foods versus SAINT Foods

At Skinny Life we have come up with two powerful acronyms to drive home the truth about how the way you eat will affect your health, energy, weight, and sense of well-being. As the new you develops new eating habits, let's redefine what food is for our bodies. Let's start with the definition of *food*:

1. Any nourishing substance that is eaten, drunk, or otherwise taken into the body to sustain life, provide energy, promote growth, etc.

2. More or less solid nourishment, as distinguished from liquids

3. A particular kind of solid nourishment: *a breakfast food; dog food*

4. Whatever supplies nourishment to organisms: *plant food*[11]

Notice the word *nourish* in each of the definitions. The acronym THIEF is a descriptive reminder of the foods that steal your health and don't really nourish your body. THIEF foods provide little to no nourishment and often create more havoc than good. At Skinny Life we believe it's time to stop considering them as food for our bodies. (You will find a list of these foods in appendix A.)

THIEF foods steal your health:

- **They**
- **Highjack**
- **Important**
- **Endocrine**
- **Functions**

Your body's response to THIEF foods will be low energy, lack of focus, fatigue, decreased immune response, increased weight issues, lower libido, and serious health issues including metabolic syndrome, diabetes, heart disease, arthritis, and other inflammation diseases.

In contrast, SAINT foods give you a lifetime of health and are:

- **S**atisfying
- **A**ctive
- **I**deal
- **N**atural
- **T**herapeutic

When you eat SAINT foods, you bless your body with great health for a lifetime! Nature has designed SAINT foods to provide high levels of energy and nutrition without being easily converted to body fat. Your body's response to SAINT foods is improved stamina, mental clarity, lower weight, and more balanced moods and hormones.

We don't need to fight our weight imbalance; we need to heal it. You can eat as many SAINT foods as you want because those foods work *with* your body chemistry. (You will find a list of these foods in appendix B.) The difference is, each time you eat these foods that work with your hormonal chemistry, you will discover several things:

- You'll feel much more satisfied after eating and for a longer period of time.
- You'll stop craving THIEF foods.
- Your energy, health, and sense of well-being will begin to vastly improve.

 **Skinny Life Bottom Line:** We don't need to fight our weight imbalance; we need to heal it.

## You Call That "Food"?

If you look in many lunchboxes of children all across the country, a lot of what you'll find is not food. Whenever I joined my daughters for lunch at their grade school, I just couldn't help but notice what the other kids were eating. Honestly, it made me a bit squeamish! Most of it was a collection of prepackaged concoctions with unrecognizable ingredients, preservatives, and sugar. I mentally calculated all of those grams of sugar as the kids pulled out gummy fruit snacks, cereal bars with deceptively nutritious-sounding names, a jelly-and-white-bread sandwich with a little smear of peanut butter, and a fruit juice drink to top it off. What these sugars, starches (which turn to sugar immediately in the body), and processed foods do to a growing body and brain is anything but nourishing, especially when we're fooling ourselves into thinking they're providing real energy and nutrition.

Too much sugar in the body is dangerous and most kids today get far too much of it. Where is the real nutrition that feeds growing bodies and developing minds? It's all but completely absent.

Try putting your kids on a whole-food diet using primarily SAINT foods and you will see vast improvements in their sustained energy and attention span. Many health care professionals are concerned about the destructive nature of sugar in the body, and research is finding that sugar may become highly addictive. Joseph Schroeder, associate professor of psychology and director of the Behavioral Neuroscience Program at Connecticut College, found in studies with rats that eating Oreos activated more neurons in the brain's "pleasure center" than drug abuse.[12]

As you shore up your own eating habits as part of the new you, you may also be able to bring the family along! If not, do it for yourself.

It's important to remember that the problem is not only what we're putting in our bodies when we eat these refined, sugary, starchy foods, many of which are also loaded with dangerous trans fats. The problem also lies in what we're not getting! If we let THIEF foods use up our appetite, mealtime, or snack time instead of letting SAINT foods fill us with delicious vitamins, minerals, proteins, and enzymes, then we are missing those important things in our bodies. We become deficient in what we really need.

If you've been relying on THIEF foods out of convenience, trust yourself and have no fear about committing instead to SAINT foods. Once you start eating whole, delicious foods, you'll begin to wonder how or why you ever ate the processed stuff!

Calories become almost irrelevant when you focus on making sure your body has plenty of good food from the proper sources. That nourishing food will trigger events that allow your body to naturally convert the food into usable energy, to distribute the energy to the places in need of it, and then to spark a feeling of fullness to shut off hunger. When you live on SAINT foods the Skinny Life way, your weight and metabolism will balance and become healthy.

When you live the Skinny Life, you will look at THIEF foods not as real foods but as an occasional treat or splurge. Once you've become a Skinny Life eater, eating a doughnut once in a while will not be a big deal because your body will be in healthy hormonal balance. When you do eat that occasional splurge, there are some tricks we'll teach you to lessen the negative impact in your body. After living the Skinny Life way, most people discover that THIEF foods that used to seem so appealing don't even taste good anymore. Skinny Lifers find it easy to avoid or walk away from them after a small bite. Now that's powerful, intentional living!

You can see why chronic dieters often look at food as the enemy. First, most diets tell you to eat less than your hunger tells you to eat. Then once you've trained your metabolism to slow down from too few calories, when you eat "normally" again you gain more weight than ever. That scenario would scare anyone! But in the Skinny Life, the new you understands that food is your friend. Eating as the new you means you love foods more than you ever have. The key is that you love the foods that love you back—not the ones that will destroy your health and longevity!

## Heal Your Body and Balance Critical Hormones

In discussions about weight and health, you may have heard about a couple of hormones: leptin and insulin. It's important to understand the crucial role these superstar regulating hormones play in your body's metabolic function.

Your body secretes insulin in response to the foods you eat—especially carbohydrates, sugars, and starches—to control blood-sugar levels after a meal. Insulin's job is to distribute glucose to your cells for energy. When your body gets too many carbohydrates, especially simple sugars, your pancreas responds to the rising blood sugar by pumping out more insulin. Eventually, your cells become resistant to it. There is simply nowhere for the all the extra glucose to go. The result? Metabolic syndrome, which is another way of saying that the cells in your body are ignoring your insulin. Your pancreas can no longer keep up with the demand, so it gives up. Once your pancreas has exhausted itself, it will stop producing insulin altogether, making it impossible for your body to break down sugar. At this point things are completely out of whack. Now your blood sugar will rise out of control, and you've got diabetes.

Leptin is the satiety (satisfaction) hormone, which regulates the

> Love the foods that love you back—not the ones that will destroy your health and longevity!

amount of fat your body stores by adjusting the sensation of hunger and energy expenditures. Blood sugar is taken up by fat cells, activating the metabolism, in turn producing the hormone leptin. Leptin now enters the blood and begins traveling up to the brain. The more you eat, the more insulin you make and the more leptin you make. When your body is hormonally in balance, your fat cells produce leptin to tell your body you're full and to tell your body to burn calories and fat as energy. When insulin has too much blood sugar to deliver to cells and the cells don't need any sugar, insulin stimulates the production of triglycerides, which can become stored fat. This is how you gain weight.

As triglycerides elevate in your blood, they get in the way of leptin's traveling to your brain. As a result, you eat more than you need to because you don't get a full signal to stop, a problem called leptin resistance. This makes it more likely you will gain weight. Studies have shown that overweight or obese people have plenty of leptin in their bloodstreams; their bodies and brains have just stopped registering it![13] Too many THIEF foods have created chaos, mixed signals, and a functional breakdown within the body.

Your body is perfectly designed so that when you eat, it knows just what to do to balance itself out. When you eat SAINT foods, your body stays in this beautifully balanced state, efficiently processing what you feed it. What interrupts that critical hormonal balance of insulin and leptin responses are THIEF foods.

 **Skinny Life Bottom Line:** Your body is perfectly designed so that when you eat, it knows just what to do to balance itself out.

# When Fasting Is the Best Option

A meal is never more important than you or your body. Clients say, "Oh I was out running around and having such a busy day, I just had to grab something. So I got some fried chicken strips, french fries, and a soda." My answer: It would be much healthier to fast through lunch and drink water than to put nutritionless stuff into your body. If you are typically getting good, regular nutrition, a greasy, deep-fried meal with disease-causing trans fats and a sugar rush causes more harm to your body than skipping the meal and letting your digestive system rest. If you hold yourself to this standard, then you will break the mental excuse program that makes you say, "I guess I have to eat junk food today because I have no choice." Now you have a choice. Fast through lunch, drink lots of water, and eat a healthy dinner.

Fasting also gives your body a chance to rebalance any hormone overloads. If you fasted through a meal once or twice a week, it would actually be good for you.[14] After you begin the practice of either eating healthy or fasting, then your smart, resourceful mind will begin to plan ahead for those times when you are busy and running around. You will start to carry with you little bags of almonds, protein bars, low-fat string cheese, carrot and celery sticks, and apples. It isn't difficult or time-consuming to make sure you have these things around. Remember, you're integrating the Skinny Life into every aspect of your lifestyle, from the way you think to the way you shop to the way you look at foods to the way you honor your body only with the best foods. With the fasting rather than junking option, Skinny Lifers quickly become experts at preparedness.

Note: Always check with a doctor before beginning a fast or establishing a fasting routine.

## Skinny Life Simple Food Rules

The following simple Skinny Life rules will form the basis of your eating habits and choices. Once you understand what foods accomplish in your body, then knowing what, when, and how much to eat will be a snap!

### Rule #1: Eliminate White Carbs

This category represents the worst of the THIEF foods. My mother was far ahead of her time on this issue. While my friends' mothers pulled out lily-white Wonder Bread to make their children's sandwiches, my mother was loading whole wheat into a stone grinder and then mixing the flour with water, natural sea salt, and some good oils to bake up the loaves she sliced for our sandwiches. Mom knew forty years ago that white flour was not good for the body.

You see, to make white flour, the wheat kernels get stripped of their bran layer, a process that removes all the fiber, minerals, and vitamins. The naturally brown flour then gets whitened via a chlorine bleach–type chemical. Studies now show that the chemical that makes white flour look white forms a substance called *alloxan*, which destroys the beta cells of your pancreas, possibly contributing to diabetes. In fact, scientists have known of the alloxan-diabetes connection for years from tests with lab rats. Bleached white flour is almost always contaminated with alloxan.[15] Most consumers obviously aren't aware, which is probably why they keep buying the white tortillas, pastries, buns, biscuits, and bread!

Combine alloxan-tainted white flour with bleached white sugar and white table salt, as many recipes call for, and you create a dangerous recipe for your pancreas. In 2008, *Diabetologia* published an article about how scientists closely examined how alloxan caused diabetes in animals.[16] Earlier they also found that children with insulin dependent diabetes had significantly higher levels of Alloxan in their blood than non-diabetic kids. It's quite easy to extrapolate that those kids probably consumed larger amounts of white-flour products.

But white flour is not the only white carb culprit. White sugar, white rice, the white breading on foods, and most of the stripped-down corn flour products from cereals to chips are all no-nos. In addition to chemical processing, these whites are stripped of most of their fiber and nutrients and cause a glycemic overload in your body, which in turn causes your insulin to spike, shooting you way past your target metabolic zone. That means your calories turn to fat.

With all of the good things to eat, there's just no reason to eat any more white carbs. Trust me, once you're off refined white starches and sugars, you won't miss them. My father-in-law was a baker. When my husband, Mark, and I started dating, I realized he was addicted to white flour and white-sugar baked goods. There wasn't a pastry, muffin, roll, cookie, or doughnut he ever wanted to say no to. Mark was one of my toughest clients!

But over time, as he kept listening to the Skinny Life principles, he saw that these sugary, starchy whites were making him prediabetic. He realized if he really cherished his health, this was a lifestyle change he needed to make. After living on SAINT foods for several years now, he has discovered that looking great, feeling great, and honoring his body feels *so* much better than the momentary carb fix he used to get from eating pastries!

Therefore Rule #1 is this: always pass on the whites! Substitute brown rice, whole grain pasta, or legumes like lentils or beans. Reach for low-sugar fresh fruit, fresh crunchy vegetables, seeds, whole-grain rice cakes and crackers, and nuts. For a list of white-carb foods to avoid, see appendix A.

### Rule #2: Avoid High Fructose Corn Syrup

At one point the food industry portrayed high fructose corn syrup (HFCS) as a healthful alternative to white sugar. But science started connecting HFCS to diabetes, and the food industry started replacing it in their products with regular sugar (sucrose) and advertising the products as if they were superior to HFCS. As clever as the marketing was, research shows that the two sweeteners are effectively identical. Refined sugar is a 50/50 mixture of fructose and glucose. High fructose corn syrup, as it is most commonly consumed, is 55 percent fructose, 45 percent glucose.[17] It is what is mostly used in soft drinks and other refined sugary snacks. Fructose is almost twice as sweet as glucose, so the more fructose in a substance, the sweeter it will be. Both refined sugar and high fructose corn syrup end up as a glucose/fructose combo in our guts, and our bodies react the same way to both.

Luc Tappy, a researcher at the University of Lausanne in Switzerland, found in a 2010 review of the relevant science that HFCS and other sources of sugar are *both* pure sugar and they both create equal havoc in the body system.[18]

As soon as you start to overeat sugars your liver converts them into fat, raises LDL cholesterol, and metabolic syndrome follows. Colorado State University biochemist Michael Pagliassotti, who conducted extensive animal studies, says that sugars "may have rapid, direct effects on the liver."[19]

Again, avoid all white and processed sugars like table sugar and HFCS and stay away from the bleached, white, refined wheat- and corn-flour products. There are hundreds of better things to eat—and we're going to talk about those now!

### Rule #3: Protein Means a Pro-Lean You

Not only is protein delicious and satisfying, but protein in most forms is really good for your body and your long-term health. Including protein at every meal and snack is a must for the new you. This habit will help you achieve your Skinny Life best in many ways.

- Protein takes longer to digest than carbohydrates and fats. Your metabolism has to burn more energy to digest protein, and who doesn't love a faster metabolism? Faster metabolism translates into a lower set point when sustained over time. Yes, you can heal your body from its old dieting ways!
- When eating protein you'll find you get full faster and stay satisfied for much longer.
- Protein provides the cellular structure for your body, including the structural components of body tissues such as muscle, bones, skin, hair, and collagen.[20]
- Protein is a power-packed source of energy your muscles

need. Studies show that most women do not get adequate amounts of protein to maintain healthy muscle tissue, especially as they reach age thirty and older.[21]

When I break down this information for clients, they're usually surprised at how much protein they need to eat for optimal health. This is why I say that when you're eating the Skinny Life way, you'll switch from a deprivation eating model to an abundance eating model. How wonderful to focus on making sure you are getting ideal amounts all of these delicious, health-promoting foods each day!

So how much is the right amount of protein? There is a spectrum of recommendations from multiple credible sources, ranging from the US Department of Agriculture to the Mayo Clinic.[22] The USDA recommends around .36 grams of protein per pound of body weight, but that recommendation is only to *prevent a loss* of existing muscle tissue. When you're embarking on a journey to change your body composition and create more lean muscle mass, most weight-loss professionals recommend .5 to 1 gram per day. I recommend women that women get about .5 grams per pound of healthy, lean body mass, and a moderately active man should be getting around .7 or .8

> When you're eating the Skinny Life way, you'll switch from a deprivation eating model to an abundance eating model.

per pound. Say you are a 270-pound woman whose goal weight is 155: you would eat as much protein each day as it takes to support a healthy, lean, 155-pound, moderately active woman, which would be 77.5 grams of protein per day on average. It's fine if some days you get 86 grams and others you might get 67. The point is, you will consistently be feeding your body the protein that supplies the building blocks required to create healthy tissue—which results in a higher metabolism.

As you engage in more muscle-building activities or become significantly more active, you may need to increase your protein consumption to prevent muscle loss. An easy way to calculate protein needs for a very active person is round it off to 1 gram of protein per pound of body weight (or desired body weight). Protein has a minimal effect on blood glucose levels, which means it does not spike your blood sugar. That's because utilization of protein in your body happens slowly and evenly over a long time period, allowing your body to feel satisfied for much longer.[23]

Protein is very low in natural sugars. These low-to-no-sugar nutritional powerhouses are a huge plus for your metabolism and your digestive tract.

There are so many delicious ways to use healthy cuts of fish, chicken breast or thigh meat, turkey breast, lean cuts of beef and pork, and eggs (I like two whole eggs with two or three whites) to make your eating adventurous and satisfying. You'll find interesting ways to combine proteins with healthy, slow-release carbs and vegetables to create optimal enjoyment at mealtimes. The trick is to combine healthy animal proteins with high-protein, slow-burning carbs like legumes, including red beans, black beans, lima beans, pinto beans, white beans, lentils, soybeans, kidney beans, or garbanzo beans, oatmeal or quinoa, or Ethiopian teff grain, which is a wonderful grain similar to quinoa but smaller in size and very high in protein, calcium, and magnesium, as well as other critical minerals. Teff is also gluten-free for people with gluten intolerance or celiac disease.

When you cut out the starchy white carbs that cause you to store fat, you can replace them with small servings of one of these slow-release carb and vegetable protein options to get a combination that burns fat and provides long-lasting energy. If you are a vegetarian or vegan, you can eat meals that combine these slow-burn carb and protein foods with non-meat proteins like tofu, Greek yogurt, or tempeh.

The key to changing your eating habits is to make sure your new ones can last a lifetime. This means getting enough high-quality calories and nutrition to satisfy your hunger and your nutritional needs. Your new Skinny Life eating habits will give you sustained energy. Protein, and the slow-release high-protein carbohydrate combination of legumes and other whole grains, balances the nutritional feed to cells consistently with no spikes or crashes. When your blood sugar is spiking and crashing it causes mood and hormonal swings, and depression.

Remember, the Skinny Life isn't about counting calories or short-term food restriction. It is a healthy-eating lifestyle that can last a lifetime. The list of SAINT foods in appendix B will help you shop for the things you need to keep on hand for the healthiest, happiest new you.

### Rule #4: Green Is Lean

To be optimally healthy and fit, you'll find a powerful food source in green vegetables. They contain vitamins, minerals, enzymes, and micronutrients that our bodies readily absorb and desperately need. They are also loaded with fiber, which allows our food to be absorbed more slowly, keeping our blood sugar and that ever-important metabolic hormonal balance in check.

If you didn't grow up eating green vegetables and don't yet know they're delicious, check out some of the easy Skinny Life tips and recipes at SkinnyLife.com. I promise that the more you integrate these into your eating, the more you will begin to crave them. My mother insisted on our having at least two vegetables with every meal and one of them had to be leafy green or raw.

Leafy greens are available everywhere. Farmers' markets and grocery stores are making them easier to find than ever. You can locate many choices of washed, bagged lettuce and spinach. Many greens come in a salad kit that's easy to prepare. (Just make sure to avoid dressings that contain high fructose corn syrup or sugars. I often use half of the dressing provided in the kit and squeeze lemon or lime over the top and toss.)

It was such fun to host my brother-in-law, Bailey, recently at our home. My husband's oldest brother has been a foreigner to healthy eating for far too long. One of his mantras was "If I can't take it out of a package and throw it in the microwave, I don't eat it!" Even though eating vegetables and salad was unusual for Bailey, I prepared a different salad to go with our meals each night. We ate dishes like multicolored cabbage salads with shredded carrots, cilantro, green onions, and slivered almonds, and mixed kale with lemon dressing and fresh Parmesan cheese. Much to my surprise he *devoured* a huge plate of salad with his dinner each evening, commenting on how delicious it was. I was pleased and relieved as he eagerly listened to my instructions on how to keep up the habit at home for himself. Bailey had lost his wife to cancer several years before, and we talked about the importance of feeding our bodies food that is naturally encoded to help prevent disease and to create optimum health. When we look at our plates of food at mealtimes, we should be sure that half or more is filled with a variety of delicious fresh vegetables.

> When we look at our plates of food, we should be sure that half or more is filled with delicious fresh vegetables.

Other green vegetables include cabbage, broccoli, cauliflower (can be white or green), Brussels sprouts, green beans, green peas, asparagus, and zucchini. If you're just getting used to eating greens, try sautéing them lightly in olive oil, garlic, and sea salt and then squeezing on some lemon; this makes any vegetable irresistible. Make sure not to overcook them—just sauté to a tender crisp so that the vitamins and enzymes aren't destroyed. It's also important to eat a large share of your veggies raw. Raw vegetables have live enzymes, which aid digestion and metabolism.

In the Skinny Life way of eating, you can eat *as much as you want* of these vegetables when they're prepared as I've described! There are other nonstarchy vegetables in a rainbow of colors that you can eat ample amounts of as well, including yellow, green, and red peppers; purple and yellow cauliflower, yellow squash, tomatoes, cucumbers, and eggplant. A more complete list is provided for you in appendix B. Finding ways to combine these delicious and nutritious eats in salsas and toppings combined with enticing flavors of fresh herbs like cilantro, basil, oregano, parsley, dill, and garlic will have you craving these guilt-free, health-promoting concoctions! You'll be amazed at how much you begin to enjoy cucumbers, broccoli, and celery with a dab of low-fat sour cream dip, or tomatoes with some thin slices of fresh mozzarella sprinkled with sea salt.

You can try all of the fabulous low-fat dressing sprays. My favorite dressing is to drizzle balsamic vinegar, olive oil, lemon, sea salt, and fresh pepper over my raw salads and veggies. Do this enough and you will start to crave these colorful, flavorful snacks over that sugary, starchy stuff that was sure to make you old and sick. You need lots of fresh raw veggies each day, and eating a variety of them is the best way to get the full spectrum of nutrition you need.

### Rule #5: Good Fats Are Good

For many years popular diet regimens taught people to stay away from fats because doctors believed that too many fats caused weight gain. But the results from low-fat diets were not what experts expected. People actually started getting heavier! For the past ten or so years, many new scientific studies have been conducted to get to the truth when it comes to low-fat versus low-carb meals.

The basic conclusion of those studies across the board is: fats aren't bad! They're not only good for us, but they're also essential components of maintaining a healthy body and brain. Most health professionals have now accepted the new evidence that says a low-carb diet (higher in fat and protein) is a much better option to maintain health and to treat obesity and other chronic, Western diseases.

In a recent Harvard study, Dr. David Ludwig found that in two groups eating exactly the same calories, the group that had the low-fat diet (which meant it was higher in sugars and starches) ended up with a slower metabolism. In the study, if you were given a high-fat, high-protein diet with exactly the same calories as the low-fat, high-carb group, the metabolism boost was equivalent to approximately an hour of exercise![24]

This is just more evidence that if you swap out sugars and starches for good-quality fats and protein, it's the equivalent of adding exercise to your routine. You can see why good fats are a really important part of the SAINT food lineup. So skip the handful of pretzels and instead grab a handful of pistachios as your afternoon snack. You'll feel much more satisfied and reap the benefits in how your body starts to shape up with these smart eating choices.

### Rule #6: Culture Your Eating with Fermented Foods

There has been resurgence in popularity and awareness about a category of foods that ancient cultures used to create superior health and digestion. From ancient Rome to Old World India, people have consumed fermented foods like sauerkraut and soured (kefir) milk as sources of natural, body-friendly bacterial flora called probiotics. Historically, Asians have enjoyed pickled fermentations of cabbage, turnips, eggplant, cucumbers, onions, squash, and carrots, and they consume these fermented treats for digestion and gut balance. Korean cuisine often includes kimchi, which is a concoction of fermented cabbage with garlic.

These friendly bacteria are critical to the highest functioning of our bodies. From top to bottom, they not only aid in digestion, but the probiotic flora found in these foods can help keep your immune system strong. Researchers have found that lean people have a higher amount of these good bacteria called probiotics in their system and lower amounts of bad bacteria. The probiotics found in fermented foods help keep the gut in balance with more beneficial bacteria, which colonize and take over the gut environment so that the bad bacteria can't get a stronghold. The association between higher amounts of friendly flora and having a leaner body is significant in your journey to achieving and keeping a lean, healthy body.

When you live the Skinny Life way, it's important to know what people who seem naturally lean and fit do. You'll usually find that they're more aware of these little things that make a huge difference in health, weight, and fitness.

Remember, not all calories are the same. There are calories that support your optimum health and weight, and those that destroy it! Swap out sugar

> Focus on high-quality, whole food and your brilliantly designed body takes care of itself.

and starch for good proteins and fats like olive oil, avocados, seeds and nuts of all kinds, grass-fed beef or bison, and wild salmon. Fill yourself with a large variety of delicious vegetables, low-sugar fruits, and flora-rich fermented foods each day. Focus on high-quality, whole food, with its natural healing properties, and your brilliantly designed body takes care of itself.

## Retrain Your Palate; Listen to Your Body

There will be an adjustment period in eating as the new you. You may be switching from eating for convenience to eating for health. You may be replacing starches and sugars with fresh vegetables and high-value proteins. Suddenly you're prioritizing the health of your precious body, and it may take time for your palate to adjust.

As you dive in, get to know your veggies and all of the fun, easy combinations, sauces, and salsas, and dishes you can make from them. You will be amazed at how easy it becomes. You throw the stuff in your cart at the store, and then every time you're hungry, you take five minutes to wash, chop, slice, and eat. (You may prefer to prepare the foods all at once so they're easy to grab later.) After a while you realize preparing whole, healthy foods is actually easy!

And when you feel hungry, ask yourself: Are you truly in need of energy, or are you just feeling a habitual signal to eat because of stress or sensory stimulation like the smell or sight of something cooking? Also listen to your body to find out when it's full. There is a spot in the lower esophagus that begins to close off when you have fed your body enough. People with weight issues have learned over time to ignore that signal completely and instead keep relying on their sensory signals like smell and taste. They keep eating what their bodies are desperately trying to tell them they don't need.

The more you practice these simple rules of eating, the more natural and effortless they become. Not only that, but your mind will find ways to come up with the perfect eating choices for you in every situation, whether you're at home, out to dinner, on the go, or with friends.

This new relationship with food will give you a sense of emotional freedom from weight and body issues. The path to that freedom is available for everyone, right now!

## Skinny Life Toolbox

### It's Pantry Cleaning Time!

At the back of the book I've included a list of the THIEF foods and SAINT foods. This is a tool we're going to continue to use over and over again as we live in Skinny Life freedom. I'd like you to get a big garbage bag and carefully go through your refrigerator, food cabinets, and pantry, looking for any THIEF foods that are sitting in your kitchen ready to steal your health. Have some fun with this exercise as you grab those things off the shelves; toss them in your trash bag and say, "You will not get between me and my greatest health *ever again!*" When you're finished with that task, copy the list of the wonderful SAINT foods and plan a shopping trip to the grocery store. As you shop for these foods, really focus on the terrific qualities of each and every one of them. Connect to the process. Let yourself feel so *good* that you are deliberately planning and implementing your perfect health and fitness plan!

# Affirmations

I feed myself the highest-quality nutrition
so that I am satisfied.

I am eating food for my greatest health value and
nutrition, not to soothe my stress or emotions.

I listen to my body's natural signals and discern true
hunger from other types of stimuli.

I make it my business to be consciously aware
of the nutrient values in foods and provide
my body with only the best.

*No more empty calories!* White, nutritionless sugars and
starches are no longer allowed into my strong,
healthy, gorgeous body.

I am eating vegetables, nuts, and high-quality proteins
that keep my blood sugar at steady, healthy levels.

Eating the Skinny Life way helps me keep
my metabolic fires burning brightly for
my greatest health, energy, and fitness.

I would rather do a water fast through
a meal than eat food that does
more harm than good.

I am eating the greens that give me vitamins,
minerals, micronutrients, and fiber that make
my cells healthy and my body feel great!

Protein is my friend. I eat high-quality proteins
throughout the day to keep my blood sugar stable
and my energy and stamina strong and steady.

I eat within an hour of waking to get
my thermic burn started.

## 10

# The New Me: My Movement

There is a reason God made you with muscles and joints. He wants you to move! As modern culture becomes so efficient that we can conduct massive communication and business by moving only ten steps from our beds to our computers, many people are falling short on meeting the body's need to move. Unlike our forebears, we don't have to hitch the horse to the wagon to get our dealings done. A growing number of people in the workforce are freelancers or employees who work from home. These conveniences allow a lot of efficiencies in our lives and our work but could be degrading our bodies and health.

So how do we take care of our bodies' need for healthy movement when we don't even have to walk from the car into the office and out again to bring home the bacon? (That would be the low-fat turkey bacon, of course.)

Since our modern environment doesn't demand that we move much, we need to provide our bodies with adequate movement that supports our vital bodily functions and health. The only way we have to use the food calories we put in is to participate in enough movement to burn them as energy.

You can find hundreds of reasons to include healthy activity and movement in your life. According to the Mayo Clinic, exercise helps elevate mood, fight disease, improve your sex life, promote better sleep, boost your daily energy level, and of course manage your weight.[1] Wow! I want all of that, don't you? Still not convinced? Exercise burns the calories you consume, increases brain function, strengthens your muscles, and supports your joints.

One of the best parts of living the Skinny Life is how fun it becomes to move your body again. If you're at the stage where exercise seems like a chore, like a dreaded assignment you wish you could get motivated about, then bear with the process. *Getting started is half the battle.* The Skinny Life approach is all about making healthy movement enjoyable. I don't expect you to pack up and get ready for the gym every other day, forcing yourself to figure out how to use all of those machines. If you like the idea of going to the gym and have a membership or can easily get one, that's great. But if you're like most people, who has time for fancy gyms and trainers? With Skinny Life, they're not necessary. I'm going to teach you how to fit fat-busting, metabolism-revving movement into your daily life.

 **Skinny Life Bottom Line:** The Skinny Life approach is all about making healthy movement enjoyable.

## Your Risks Go Up When You Sit Down

*Exercise and Sport Sciences Reviews* published important research on the dangers to our health of too much sitting. The paper differentiated between *too much sitting* and *too little exercise*, with exercise being a focused period of intense bodily exertion. Even if we exercise for an hour a day, we will not avoid the negative effects of sitting the rest of the day![2]

Their scientific findings on this correlation between sedentary behavior and compromised health have been greatly expanded in the last ten years. In January 2010, British experts linked prolonged periods of sitting to a greater likelihood of disease.[3] Researchers in Australia found that every hour you spend watching television links you to an 18 percent increase in the risk of dying from cardiovascular disease.[4] One of the intriguing findings from the studies is that incorporating activity breaks in sedentary time had a beneficial effect on metabolism. In one group studied, more sedentary time also increased the chance the subject had a larger waist circumference and higher triglyceride levels.[5]

One study talked about the "Active Couch Potato phenomenon," which meant that time spent watching TV had negative metabolic consequences, even for people who participated in regular physical exercise that would qualify them as a lower heart-disease risk. In other words, no matter how hard you worked out earlier in the day, too much sitting over a period of time is still a problem for your body. The point is to get up and deliberately weave some active movement into your sitting periods.[6]

The American College of Sports Medicine and the American Heart Association state that the recommended amount of aerobic activity (whether moderate or vigorous) should occur *in addition* to routine activities of daily living that are of light intensity, such as self-care, casual walking, grocery shopping, walking to the parking lot, or taking out the trash. The findings indicate that for every hour of sitting, you need to take ten minutes to get up and move around.[7] (We have some great ideas on how to do this in the paragraphs below.) According to the evidence, the important thing about these tasks is that they interrupt that excessive *sitting* we're all doing! When you do those tasks, and in fact even when you stand rather than sit, your body works at a different metabolic level because of the movement and the muscle engagement that it takes to stand, walk, lift, or bend.[8]

## An Old-Fashioned Future: The Amish

Researchers looked at how technology influences activity levels in modern society. The Amish are known for their physically demanding lifestyle and for living without modern technology. Pedometers were placed on a group of Amish farmers, and their physical activities were logged for seven days. Amish men averaged about eighteen thousand steps each day and also shoveled trenches, tossed hay bales, and did other heavy lifting. The women took an average of fourteen thousand steps per day, interspersed with periods of picking fruit and vegetables, weeding, and other ways of tending to the family farm.[9]

In America, today's accepted active lifestyle standard is about ten thousand steps per day. The Amish were found to have performed six times more physical activity per day than a study of two thousand participants in twelve modernized nations and ten times more compared to mainstream respondents in Colorado.[10]

So how does all of that physical activity in the Amish community translate? Only 4 percent of the Amish population is obese as defined by a body mass index above thirty, whereas 31 percent of the US adult population is obese. The other amazing fact noted by the researchers is that the Amish ate a high-calorie, high-fat diet and still had low obesity rates![11] Thomas Sanders, director of the Nutrition, Food & Health Research Centre at King's College–London and coauthor of *You Don't Have to Diet!*, says:

We've become sedentary. We sit at our desks all day, then go home and watch TV. These days there are more people watching sports, do it yourself makeovers and gardening programs than actually doing them. And yet if we kept our calorie intake in line with our expenditure, we could all be enjoying food the way the Amish do.[12]

Dr. David R. Bassett, professor at the University of Tennessee–Knoxville and lead researcher for the Amish study, said, "The Amish were able to show us just how far we've fallen in the last 150 years or so in terms of the amount of physical activity we typically perform. . . . Their lifestyle indicates that physical activity played a critical role in keeping our ancestors fit and healthy."[13]

## Are You a Sit-a-Holic?

Every cell, organ, and system in your body depends on movement. Consider the time you spend sitting each day. By the time you work on your computer, go home to sit for dinner, and then sit to unwind on the couch, that's a big chunk of your day spent on your tush. As you begin to pay attention, you'll see that it's probably far too much inactivity to be healthy.

Take into account that most of the errands we needed to run ten or fifteen years ago to make bank deposits, drop off mail, and shop are now often accomplished when we're—ah yes—doing more sitting. Remember when you used to have to run to the hardware store to grab a flashlight? Now just click a button on your smartphone for an insta-flashlight. Online banking and shopping and phone apps make us more efficient, but more susceptible to wide thighs and unhealthy hearts. You can see how without even trying, you could become a sedentary sit-a-holic.

Develop your own sit-a-holic radar. Get in touch with that vibrant, happy, and aware new you that says, "I love and honor my body, so I will regularly find ways to move it!" If you work at home, stand up, grab a stepstool, and wipe off that dusty shelf you've been staring at for the last month. While the stepstool is in front of you, step up and down on it twenty times. Do two sets of twenty desk push-ups or a couple of sets of jumping jacks. Right then and there you've kicked up your metabolism!

If you're in the middle of a long sitting stint at the office, get up and take the long way to the restroom or the meeting. Always look for stairs, and walk up and down them a couple of times to get your metabolism burning at a higher level. If I'm stuck on a phone call for a while, I *stand* and talk. Standing engages leg and body muscles and demands energy.

## Skinny Life Toolbox

### Do You Sit Too Much?

Let's make sure you're not one of those people who is compromising your health and longevity, perhaps unknowingly, by sitting too much.

Ask yourself the following questions:

- Does my daily work involve sitting six or more hours?
- How many hours in total, working, driving, watching TV do I sit each day?
- Do I get on a project and not stand up for two, three, or more hours at a time?
- Do I feel like my environment or job demands won't allow me to get up during the day?

If you answered yes to *any* of these questions, you need to make some changes now that will pay in spades for your future health and longevity.

### Don't Automatically Accept Automation

Just because everything has been automated for us doesn't mean we have to accept it. Remember, God put you in charge of you. Technology and media have made some enhancements, but are we letting those things take over our lives, including the compromising of our precious bodies? We need to carve out boundaries and commit more time and effort toward healthy activity in lieu of more computer time or the wide variety of social media.

Since our natural opportunities for physical movement have decreased significantly, we need to be deliberate about weaving healthy activity into our daily lives. Make the choice to ride a bike or walk to a store. If you have a favorite coffee shop within a mile, try taking a stroll there on a Saturday morning.

I've even taken to doing things by hand like juicing oranges with my hand juicer rather than throwing them in the automatic juicer. Washing my own car in the sunshine rather than sitting there while I watch a machine do it. Getting my big hedge clippers and trying my own style of landscape art on the bushes rather than counting on my lawn maintenance guy to do it. When you begin substituting old-fashioned manual activities for automation, try to focus on the joy of movement in your body. Try to connect with the feeling of your arm muscles contracting and getting stronger as you squeeze those oranges or work those shears. Try to feel your whole body come alive as you decide to joyfully move through your day, not begrudging the tasks but giving thanks that you have a beautiful, healthy, strong body that can serve you so well to create order and beauty in your life.

## Combine Two Types of Exercise

A couple of different types of exercises target and support specific body and health functions.

Aerobic exercise

- is brisk physical activity that requires the heart and lungs to work harder to meet the body's increased oxygen demand;

- promotes the circulation of oxygen through the blood;
- strengthens the heart and lungs;
- causes a transformation of our breathing and resting heart rate, making it easier for us to do things like take the stairs;
- includes walking fast, jogging, hiking, swimming, biking, and my personal favorite, dancing.

Anaerobic exercise

- is any activity in which the working muscles require and utilize oxygen at a faster rate than your body can supply it;
- is essential to the functionality of our reflexes, the strength of our muscles, and the protection of our joints;
- causes small tears in the muscle that then have to rebuild themselves, which results in stronger, tighter muscles— which become fat-burning furnaces;
- includes weightlifting, sprinting, baseball, and rock climbing.

During a strength workout, "the heart's muscle tissue contracts forcefully to push the blood out. [As with] all muscles, stress causes small tears in the muscle fibers. When the body repairs those tears, muscles grow. The result is a stronger heart, not just one that's more efficient at pumping."[14] Anaerobic exercise is optimal for a daylong calorie burn.

The combination of aerobic and anaerobic exercise is essential to burning calories and improving our overall health. Experts generally agree that a combination of aerobic and anaerobic activity two or three times weekly is the perfect complement to other healthy lifestyle movements like cleaning your house, climbing the stairs, and taking out the trash. This leaves time for your body to recuperate and strengthen itself, while still keeping it in a strong metabolic zone.

## Muscles: Your Fat-Burning Furnace

Your muscles are the most active living tissue on your body, which means they demand energy. Muscles are your fat-burning, metabolic megastars! A report published by the Center for Disease Control confirms what we've taught at Skinny Life for years: people who have tried dozens of diets only to regain weight find that using muscle-strength training is a game changer. Muscles use lots of energy (calories), while fat uses very little.[15] In other words, muscle on your body works for you to stay lighter and leaner, while fat works against you.

Unfortunately we begin to lose muscle as we get older or become inactive. In fact, experts have shown that most people can lose five to seven pounds of muscle tissue per decade![16] The more muscle they lose, the more fat they gain. This becomes a very unhealthy cycle that degrades quality of life dramatically and eventually leads to serious health problems.

Power moves (movements that are high in intensity but short in duration), resistance techniques (bands and cords to challenge and strengthen your muscles), and weights lifted in various ways will help create healthy muscle-to-fat ratio in your body and promote an appropriate natural weight for you. You want to train your muscles for strength however and whenever you can. The side effect of this kind of strength training moves is that they burn more calories than other aerobic types of activities. In fact it can increase your metabolism by up to 15 percent![17] We definitely need both for different reasons, but it's critical to do power and strength moves each and every week.

Weight management is just one of the great benefits of strength training. Used regularly, strength training will cause

- an increase in bone density;
- protection from back pain;
- improvement in flexibility and balance;
- protection from diseases like arthritis, osteoporosis, heart disease, and diabetes;
- improved cognitive performance, especially as you age;
- improvements in the quality of your sleep and moods during the day.[18]

## Start Off Easy

Whenever you can, grab some hand weights—keep a set under your couch and one under your work desk. (I also like the wrist and angle weight wraps with Velcro closures.) Sneak in seven to ten different strength moves using all areas of your body. Try raising and lowering your legs and arms, bent and unbent from all different directions to feel the different muscles that are engaged when you change your body position just a little bit. (There are lots of free demonstrations on YouTube that will show you a variety of ways to do this, and you can also get more ideas, demonstrations, and daily support in our "Tips and Tricks" in the Skinny Life online membership program.) Start out with ten repetitions of each one. Gradually you can increase to two or three sets, even if you have to break it up during the day.

Don't rush the moves. You get the best benefit by moving slowly because you're forcing the muscle to be fully engaged for the full range of the movement and not relying on swinging the weight to its position.

Begin with a lower weight. Even two to five pounds is good if you've never done strength training. Later, when it becomes easy to do all of your reps, you can get a heavier weight; for now, work up slowly until you're at a weight that challenges you continuously without straining your joints. Always check with your doctor before you begin any exercise so that he or she can help you determine that you're in good condition to begin.

> There's nothing more attractive on the human body than a well-shaped muscle group.

Strength or weight training offers many wonderful benefits, but most amazing is how you begin to feel about yourself after you've gotten in the habit of doing it. Skinny Lifers who felt before as if their body shapes and fitness were on a downhill slide have been astounded at how good they start to look in a fairly short period of time. There's nothing more attractive on the human body than a well-shaped muscle group. The more toned muscle you have, the more fit and youthful you look and feel. It's one of the ways to feel truly powerful, strong, and capable in your own body.

## Pain Is No Gain—Make It Fun!

So often I've heard, "I was good with my gym membership for a while and then I just couldn't do it anymore." Or "I had a trainer but then I fell off the wagon." Let's face it. Who's going to continue doing something they hate? Getting in touch with the ways you love to move will help eliminate failure and keep you enjoying and even craving healthy movement for the rest of your life.

Physical activity should never be about suffering, pain, or punishment. Healthy movement should be about celebrating the way your beautiful body was made. What a gift that God designed us to walk, move, and explore our world. People were not designed for sitting all day. That kind of physical confinement isn't healthy for the body, mind, or spirit! He didn't craft us to sit like rocks; he designed us to dance through life!

 **Skinny Life Bottom Line**: Physical activity should never be about suffering, pain, or punishment.

In fact, researchers at Cornell University wanted to find out why some people lose weight when they start a new exercise routine and others do not. The research involved studies of two groups of adults. The adults were led on about a mile-and-a-half walk around a small lake. One group was told they were going to take a fun, scenic walk; the other, an exercise walk. In the first study the groups were given lunch after they completed the walk. Those participants who believed they had just taken an exercise walk ate 35 percent more chocolate pudding for dessert than those who believed they had been on a fun walk. Interestingly, the pudding eaters did not eat any more vegetables or salad, just the extra dessert.[19]

In the second study, two groups were given a midafternoon snack after their walks. Those thinking they had taken an exercise walk ate twice as much—206 more calories than the others! The finding was clear. People who look at activity as exercise often think they have an excuse to use sweets and desserts to reward themselves after.[20] When we begin to look at our active movement as a well-deserved break rather than exercise, it becomes a fun reward. Ask yourself how many times have you've rewarded yourself with something sweet or indulgent because you convinced yourself exercise was tough or difficult. That's exactly why so many people never lose weight when they start a new exercise regimen. They turn around and add junk foods right back into the mix, sometimes causing more weight to be gained than lost!

> Use your mind to frame healthy movement as something fun and even a bit indulgent.

That's why in the Skinny Life philosophy we say, "No more pain and punishment." We want you to think of your movement as a joy and a deserved break to look forward to. Use your mind to frame healthy, active movement as something fun and even a bit indulgent.

## Ideas for Fun Workouts

What is your favorite way to move your body? Did you love to dance in high school? Could you beat anyone on the tennis court? Or do you enjoy jogging on a quiet road before anyone else is up, listening to the chirping birds?

One of my clients found that she enjoyed strapping her camera into a fanny pack and running around her neighborhood. Whenever she saw something interesting or beautiful, she would snap a picture. She combined her hobby with healthy movement, which made it doubly rewarding! When people get going with the Skinny Life, those who are the best at finding ways to move that they actually enjoy stay with their exercise, get slimmer, and stay slimmer.

Living the Skinny Life means learning to use your body the way it was meant to be used. So lift, squat, jump, run, reach, push, pull, twist, and leap! Once you make a point to discover the joy in movement and being active, you'll never accept the couch-potato life again. It's simply not as much fun. In the Skinny Life world, opportunities to move, to be active, and to burn calories are all around you all the time. You just need to learn to recognize them.

Keep a list on your fridge of all the fun ways to indulge:

- Swimming
- Jumping rope
- Riding bikes
- Rollerblading
- Ice skating
- Tennis
- Walking or jogging through scenic parks
- Climbing your favorite hills or mountains

Add your own favorites!

Be sure to change it up a bit so you're never bored. Do whatever you can to increase the fun factor in your activities by playing music, watching a video, or doing a gratitude meditation as you exercise. When you embrace the "new you" mind-set of the Skinny Life, it's easy to get hooked on healthy movement. Try it and see for yourself!

## Skinny Life Toolbox

### What Activities Do You Enjoy?

Let's take a minute to get in touch with an active, happy you. I want you to think back to activities you've loved to do in your past by answering these questions:

- At what point in my life did I get the most active movement?
- How many times per week did I do the activities I loved and for how long?
- What activities brought me the greatest feelings of freedom and joy?
- What activities or sports have I done in the past that made me feel powerful, strong, and capable?
- Were there friends or family involved who made it more fun?
- What were the circumstances surrounding my favorite activities? For instance, did you:
    - love water sports as a kid because you were near a lake? (Join a local YMCA and indulge in swimming and water aerobics.)

- ice skate and snow ski because you lived in the northern climes? (Grab those blades and your kids and head out to the ice rink on weekends or after school.)
- play on a softball or basketball team? (Find a local softball league and get that glove warmed up.)
- do after-school dance classes? (How about Zumba three times a week with friends?)

Write down your answers to these questions and focus on getting in touch with the *feelings* these activities create inside you. Then latch onto those that felt the best and find ways to start bringing those things back into your life to create new, wonderful memories *and* a strong, healthy body.

## Get Up and Go Everywhere, Anytime

For most people, it's not practical to spend an hour each day on exercise. Many people want to be slim, fit, and healthy, but they just can't see a way to add one more commitment to their schedules. The good news is that you don't have to!

As you continue in your Skinny Life lifestyle, you can implement a whole-day movement strategy that allows you to get five-to-ten-minute stints of regular movement, all day long. Here are some ways to make your whole day a lot more movement-oriented.

### Work in a Workout at the Workplace

There should never be a barrier between you and movement. If you are stuck at the computer most of the day, take seven to ten minutes every hour to stand up, touch your toes, twist, bend, and do arm rotations or leg lifts. If you get stuck sitting for too long, start to clench and relax your leg, glutes, abdomen, and arm muscles as often as possible. And don't forget to stretch out those cramped muscles. Each muscle matters and adds up to a leaner you!

### Divide an Hour into Lunch-and-Move Time

Most people take an hour for lunch, but is it really necessary to sit for another hour after you've been doing that all day? Instead, break your lunchtime in half. If it's an hour, have a salad with protein and a couple of whole-grain seeded crackers for a half hour, then take a thirty-minute walk around the neighborhood. Some people like to walk first and eat second. Either way, plan it and follow through. Even if you take a half-hour lunch, fifteen minutes of fresh air and brisk walking will refresh your mind, pump your metabolism, and clear your head for the rest of your workday.

### Stand for Something

Who says we need to take information sitting down? In the office, you can stand and pace as you are processing your thoughts or listening on the phone. In my experience, I have found that people get more productive when they intersperse sitting with standing or pacing.

### Walk-and-Talk Sessions

Meetings don't have to take place inside. Instead of facing each other across the desk, ask the people you're meeting with if they'll walk with you. My husband and I have found that employees and clients relax and are often more authentic when we take them outside for a stroll around our office campus during a meeting. The break refreshes and invigorates everyone, especially if they've had an intensive discussion for an hour or so. After ten minutes of fresh air and walking, they're ready to dive in and get back to work. A brisk ten-to-fifteen-minute walk in the middle of a long afternoon can perk you up so you're far more energized and productive for the final hours of your workday.

### Don't Just Sit There, Mom or Dad

Why should kids be the only ones who are getting the healthy benefits of exercise outdoors? If you find yourself spending a fair amount of sitting time at soccer practice or even taking kids to the park to play, resist the urge to read a book or chat with other parents. This is a perfect time for you to get in some healthy movement while the kids are preoccupied. Take a power walk around the ballpark while you enjoy nature. Lift your knee to the opposite elbow while crunching your abs a bit as you watch the kids scramble up the monkey bars. Do forty reps of this for two or three sets and you'll be breathing hard like the little ones! There's just no reason to spend great outdoor opportunities like this doing more sitting. Get up and move!

### Commute Time Could Be Move Time

If you live far from work and have to drive or take a bus, consider parking farther away and walking the last ten or fifteen minutes or getting off at the bus stop before yours. If you take a crowded train, choose to stand instead of fighting for the seats. Activity choices that take just ten or fifteen minutes in your day might end up adding ten or fifteen years to your life!

### Enjoy Guilt-Free TV

During those favorite television programs, try moving. If that treadmill has been collecting dust in the garage, clean it up and bring it in. You can get in a solid hour of walking, relieve your stress, and not even miss your number-one show! Try some push-ups, crunches, and leg lifts.

### Rekindle Your Love Life

Couples often get too busy for each other as life's demands begin to get in the way of love. Reconnecting with your spouse and burning calories is definitely a win-win. Having sex burns about 150 to 250 calories per half hour.[21] Sexual activity also has a number of great health benefits, and studies show that more frequent sex creates greater longevity.[22] The great thing is it's very enjoyable, free, and creates a deeper bond between husband and wife. Let your love machine become the ultimate exercise machine!

### Be a Kid Again

Playing with your kids can not only create some of the best bonding times, it is also an easy way to clock in some serious fat-burning, muscle-building time. Grab a basketball and shoot some hoops with the kids for a half hour before dinner. Pick up that old tennis racket and walk or jog with your family to your local tennis courts. Who cares if you're not an expert player? Hitting the ball and running across the court will let you laugh, learn, and sweat together.

Be creative. This is time very well spent!

Quite frankly, with the crazy schedule my husband and I maintain, using these simple opportunities is often the only way to keep healthy movement going in our lives. On days we have more time, like a weekend, my husband and I choose a different adventure like a new bike route, a different hike, or depending on the season, we head up to the mountains for some snow skiing or to the ocean for some kayaking.

If you need more ideas of how to incorporate activity and movement into your daily life, the Skinny Life Total Living virtual program (www.Skinnylife.com) gives you two video tips and tricks per week that include great, easy power moves to fit in anywhere in your day!

## Create a New Reward System

When you do get out and begin to feel the successes of your efforts to stay fit, active, and healthy, reward yourself. Not with sugar-laden cupcakes or fast food. Instead, set aside a little cash (maybe the money you used to spend on junk food) and use it for your personal reward system. Ladies, when you work out consistently all week long, take the extra cash and treat yourself to a pedicure or a fun new top to hug your lean curves. Men, when you've integrated some great workouts into your week, treat yourself to a round of golf. You'll find that by replacing your health-robbing habits with life-sustaining principles and memorable experiences, you have not only beat the overeating bug, but you've also created a more fulfilled, enjoyable life!

When my client Mindy got her friend Ilene to join her in the Skinny Life journey, each of them created a reward "bank" (a pretty jar on their counter) to stuff a little cash every time they passed on fast food or a pastry at their favorite coffee shop, or clocked in some healthy movement time. When they had saved enough money they would pick a reward such as a moms' night out together or a deep-tissue massage at a local day spa. They found that rewarding themselves to skip bad foods and deliberately planning better, more meaningful rewards made their lives more satisfying and richer.

## Movement Helps Mind-Set

The Skinny Life journey is about treating you as a whole person. When you understand wholeness as a philosophy, you know that as you improve one area like integrating regular, healthy movement, you'll notice an automatic improvement in your mood. As your mood is more consistently moderated through healthy, happy movement, it becomes easier to control and master your eating because you're not as prone to mindless emotional binges or eating to relieve stress.

> The movement of your body can quiet your thoughts.

The movement of your body can quiet your thoughts, helping you point your focus back to positive, productive, and meaningful things. You will begin to change your identity at every level of consciousness so you ultimately become the person you want to be from the inside out.

# Affirmations

I am ready to make these important changes
in my lifestyle now.

It is time for me to make these changes for
my health, well-being, and fitness.

I am embracing a new awareness about
the importance of movement for my health.

I look for healthy ways to move my body at every
opportunity.

I enjoy feeling stronger as I do my resistance and
strengthening moves.

I enjoy the way it feels to move my body
the way God designed it to move.

I feel better and stronger every day as I become more fit.

I trust my body to do miraculous things.
That's the way God made it!

I love building my health through healthy movement.

I am ready to weave exercise and movement
into my daily activities and I embrace
each opportunity to do so.

I reward my efforts to integrate healthy movement
with a healthy reward system.

I have fun moving, being active, and challenging myself
to do things I couldn't do before.

I deserve to have the healthiest, fittest,
slimmest body possible.

I am ready now to live the Skinny Life lifestyle!

# 11

# Supplements: God's Miracles in Nature

You hear a lot about vitamins and supplements these days. Most people I've met have a limited understanding of them and wonder if they're even necessary. Let's clear up some of that confusion right now!

Vitamins are compounds we need to sustain life and health, but the human body is not capable of making these compounds. So our bodies rely on foods to provide these essential nutrients to us. The problem, many experts agree, is that food is getting less and less nutritious.

Overuse is depleting the soil in farms and fields in which food is grown.[1] The petroleum-based synthetic fertilizers used in nonorganic farming impact the beneficial microbes that naturally would exist in healthy soil. These microbes normally are there to help plants draw nutrients. When soil becomes deficient by overfertilization, the natural microbial action isn't available to make a supernutritious plant or crop.[2]

Many health experts are also concerned about the unknown consequences of using genetically modified (GMO) seeds for our food. There is no real data to prove they are safe in the long term for human consumption. The argument remains that if we modify the gene of a natural plant, it may not provide the complex cellular nutrition our cells need, or worse, may disrupt critical metabolic functions of which we're not even aware. Giant corporate food producers want to grow massive amounts of crops without dealing with insect problems, so they've created insect-resistant seeds (GMOs) to replace those seeds that before existed in a natural state. Bugs won't eat the GMO plants. Many people are not convinced these foods are really okay for human consumption. If bugs intuitively won't eat them, should we? According to experts, a large portion of our corn and soybean supply in the United States is grown from genetically engineered seeds.[3]

Some of the other major problems with our modern food supply arose from a need for convenience. We've refined and processed food so it lasts longer and is more addictive than natural whole food. In that refining process much of the nutrition is stripped away. Essential vitamins, minerals, and fatty acids are removed in this denaturing process, leaving empty calories that cause weight gain and provide little nutrition.

The United Nations Conference on Environment and Development in 1992 revealed that the level of minerals in the soil throughout the world has declined drastically in the last hundred years. The United States' farmlands showed the highest depletion of mineral content at an average of 85 percent![4]

Donald Davis and his team of researchers from the University of Texas at Austin's Department of Chemistry and Biochemistry did a landmark study on the topic, which was published in December 2004 in the *Journal of the American College of Nutrition*. They studied US Department of Agriculture nutritional data from both 1950 and 1999 for forty-three different vegetables and fruits, finding "reliable declines" in the amount of protein, calcium, phosphorus, iron, riboflavin (vitamin B2) and vitamin C over the past half century. Davis and his colleagues attribute this declining nutritional content to agricultural practices designed to improve traits (size, growth rate, pest resistance) other than nutrition.[5]

The evidence is clear: Our soils have been stripped of essential minerals. Those soils we rely on to nourish the foods that come to life are already deficient. This means our food, even when we focus on being conscious eaters, has no way of nourishing us like it used to.[6]

As an example, according to the measurements taken by the USDA back in 1914, an apple used to contain 13.5 mg of calcium, 28.9 mg of magnesium, and 4.6 mg of iron. However, according to the USDA's 1992 measurements, our depleted soil only yielded apples containing 7 mg of calcium (48.15% less), 5 mg of magnesium (82.7% less) and .18 mg of iron (96% less). And that was back in 1992.[7] According to this study, we would have to eat at least twenty-five apples to get all the nutrition our grandparents got from eating one.

A 2007 report issued by the Organic Center says, "The unintentional and largely unnoticed slippage in nutrient density has been accepted as a price of progress in boosting yields. After all, more total nutrients are harvested from a field of corn producing twice the yield, even if it means 20 percent less protein or iron per bushel."[8] So essentially we have double the food production in the same fields but the nutritional quality of the food ending up on our plates is significantly lower.

But the soil is just the beginning. On average, that already depleted apple must travel thousands of miles to your kitchen, and every minute that your food travels, it loses micronutrients due to exposure to heat, light (UVs), and air (oxidation).

With all we know today, these changes to our food supply could be creating serious effects on our health. How else is it that we have so many autoimmune disorders, food allergies, and a growing epidemic of obesity? We are the world's first generation living largely on processed or denatured foods. I would suggest we are not getting adequate amounts of the steady supply of vitamins and minerals we need that allow our bodies to function properly. Taking vitamins and supplements, then, seems like such a good idea—until you realize that most of the vitamins on the market are made synthetically and are not what your body needs either.

## Whole-Food Supplements for the Whole You

I've mentioned that I was blessed to grow up in an environment where the emphasis was on health, healing, and wellness. From the time I was born, my mother embraced clean, healthy living through movement, whole-food nutrition, and whole-food supplementation.

Her introduction to the idea of whole-food supplements arose from a very scary event. When she was pregnant with me, my dad woke up in the night to a strange sound of humming next to him.

When he reached over to touch my mother, he found her entire body as stiff as a plank of wood. She was having a grand mal seizure.

Dad called an ambulance. Mom was taken to the hospital, and after days of testing with no conclusive results, she was referred to a neurologist in the neighboring town. Interestingly, when she reached to the doctor's office, another pregnant woman was waiting to see the doctor for the same reason! The woman, Sally, had also had a grand mal seizure while pregnant. They chatted and exchanged information.

The doctor prescribed the same drug to both of them. My mother remembers the doctor telling her, "I'm not sure why you had this seizure, but I'm going to put you on this medicine for two years. Come back and see me after that."

Mom went home and called my grandmother, who said, "Don't you dare take a drug with that baby in your womb—they don't even know what's wrong with you or if it will help you. I'm coming to get you to take you to a new chiropractic, naturopathic doctor. His name is Dr. Long."

My mom was shaking as she dumped the prescription in the toilet and prepared to see this new doctor. His office was in a little town in Idaho. At Mom's appointment, Dr. Long gently adjusted her body with chiropractic techniques, did some saliva and blood testing, and gave her some whole-food supplements. He told her to come back every couple of weeks, to stay on the supplements, and she would never have another seizure. She followed Dr. Long's orders, and he was right. She never had another seizure. I was born healthy and strong, with no complications.

Fast-forward in my life to age nine, when I was taking dance lessons at Ms. Sally's dance studio. After my older sister and I jumped in the car to go home, I asked Mom, "What is wrong with Sally's son, the one who is my age? He doesn't go to regular school and he doesn't really talk." My mom explained the story of her grand mal seizure, that Sally was the woman in that neurologist's office with her, and that this boy was the baby in Sally's womb. No one will ever know for sure the cause of the young boy's challenges, but my mom was very grateful that she chose Dr. Long's natural therapy course while pregnant, which resulted in the birth of a very healthy, normal baby.

As I was growing up, Dr. Long was our family doctor. My mother would take a few of her nine kids up at a time, depending on who needed it, for chiropractic and naturopathic treatments. As Mom and the other siblings were treated, I entertained myself by reading the informational brochures Dr. Long kept on a huge rack in his office. I would read pamphlets with titles like *Adrenal Fatigue*, *Diabetes*, and *Gallstones*. It seems now like a painful way for a kid to kill time, but over the years, I started connecting to the idea that the way you fed and cared for yourself mattered a whole lot and kept you from getting some of these awful-sounding conditions. Dr. Long would remind us kids:

- Processed white sugar is bad. (Stay away from soda and candy.)
- Processed white flour is bad. (Stay away from white bread and doughnuts.)
- Supplements can correct your body's deficiencies to help it come back to its natural state of health.

- It is important to use whole-food supplements that provide the nutrition of the whole vitamin complex.

I had no way of knowing at the time that my childhood upbringing and education would continue to serve me for a lifetime and help shape the direction of my work.

**Skinny Life Bottom Line:** I started connecting to the idea that the way you fed and cared for yourself mattered a whole lot and kept you from getting some of these awful-sounding conditions.

## What is Nutritional Therapy?

Learning more about how to use nutritional therapy in your life can make a remarkable difference in your health, energy, and fitness levels. Superior supplements that have been scientifically formulated can play a big role in balancing the biochemical and physiological processes of your body.

Many of the Skinny Lifers I've worked with describe feeling as if they're starving a lot of the time, despite the fact that they are eating a lot of calories and are heavier than they should be. Studies have been done that may give us a scientific explanation for that. In a recent one published in the *Journal of the American College of Nutrition*, researchers analyzed responses of eighteen thousand Americans involved in a seven-year survey. They discovered an important relationship between how much you weigh and how many vitamins and minerals you consume. Compared to normal-weight individuals, obese adults had 5 to 12 percent lower intakes of all micronutrients across the board. Specific deficiencies were noted. Compared to normal-weight adults there was a 20 percent higher incidence of obese adults lacking in vitamin A, vitamin C, and magnesium. They were also less likely to meet recommended federal requirements for calcium, vitamin D, and vitamin E.[9]

People with higher body mass index do tend to eat foods with higher calories and lower nutrients. But research is revealing that inadequate nutrient intake may actually contribute to obesity. For instance, vitamin A is linked to regulation of fat cells and the hormones they release—and naturally could play a role in maintaining healthy body weight. In one study of middle-aged and older men, those who ate more foods with beta-carotene (the whole-food source of vitamin A) were likely to have lower measures of body fat and triglycerides (blood fat) plus lower incidence of metabolic syndrome.[10] Metabolic syndrome is a group of symptoms and risk factors that increase your chance of heart disease and diabetes.

Further research shows that vitamin D may play a role in the release of leptin, the hormone that controls our sense of hunger and how much fat is stored in the body. This vitamin plays a positive role in keeping a person's metabolic set point low. They concluded that not getting adequate amounts of this critical vitamin could have an impact on our body weight.[11]

I've found that supplementation with key nutrients can also help you feel naturally satisfied. When all your nutritional needs are being met, often that feeling of hunger subsides and it's easier to control your appetite and make more deliberate healthy choices. As I began supplementing regularly, I noticed that a lot of my cravings went away, and many of my clients discovered the same thing. That is because you are giving your body the raw materials so that you are "fed" at a cellular level. When cells are truly nourished they become satisfied, and your natural processes can function properly.

**Skinny Life Bottom Line:** When cells are truly nourished they become satisfied, and your natural processes can function properly.

## What Is a Whole-Food Supplement?

Just as the name suggests, whole-food supplements are made from concentrated whole foods. The vitamins in these supplements are biological complexes that include antioxidants, activators, enzymes, and coenzymes. And this is just what we know about what we call "vitamins." Experts agree there are many unknown factors that all must work synergistically to enable the vitamin complex to perform its role in your body. If that vitamin complex is missing some parts, it has no way of accomplishing the task it was designed for once it enters your body.

At Skinny Life we knew through our research and experience, that no matter how good we are at eating healthy SAINT foods and using healthy movement, the demands of our busy lives make it almost impossible to get all we need each day for optimum health. We also knew that even for the best eaters, our food supply has become increasingly less nutritious due to the depleted soils, pesticides, and GMOs, as we discussed earlier.

Adding some key vitamins, minerals, and other whole-food

supplements can be an important added boost to your Skinny Life journey. They can be another tool in your Skinny Life Toolbox to take care of the whole you by helping your body stay balanced, slim, and healed.

# Look for Quality Supplements

When you are choosing supplements to add to your health routine, it's important to consider quality and type of ingredients that will do your body the most good. There are some key nutritional elements that many people find difficult to eat in amounts that create optimum health. Below are some supplements I recommend as part of the Skinny Life lifestyle to attain the highest function of great health and metabolism possible.

### *Vitamins and Minerals with Whole-Food Ingredients*

We now know the health benefits of consuming whole-food nutrients. These ingredients in the diet increase the body's antioxidant capacity, fight against weight-related disease, reduce the destruction of DNA, improve immune function, and help slow the body's natural aging process.

Trying to include the USDA's recommended nine servings of fruits and vegetables daily is often difficult.[12] To offset those potential deficiencies you may consider taking a well-formulated daily supplement containing a nutrient-dense blend of whole-food vitamin complexes, antioxidants, and minerals we all need to stay alive. Look for supplements with naturally occurring phytonutrients, such as caretenoids, phytoestrogens, resveratol, and flavenoids, many of which have been studied and found to prevent disease.[13]

### *Essential Fatty Acids*

Essential fatty acids, otherwise known as omega-3 fatty acids, have become popular in recent years and for a very good reason: they positively affect virtually every system in the body. The two crucial ones are EPA and DHA, which are primarily found in certain fish. Another omega-3, ALA, comes from nuts and seeds. Fish oil, flaxseed oil, and micro-algae oils are all good sources of omega-3s.

Essential fatty acids are necessary for cognitive and neurological development but have been found to be lacking in most American diets. Omega-3s reduce the risk of heart disease, protect against stroke, lower blood pressure, and protect against aging. Other studies show flaxseed to act as an anti-inflammatory, helping those with arthritis. Flaxseed may also have anti-tumor effects.

DHA is important for brain and eye development. Research has shown it to be significant in memory, learning, and preventing neurological disorders. Numerous studies have found DHA to help protect against heart disease. Further studies show that essential fatty acids supplementation enhances the effect of a good diet, including greater weight reduction and better cardiovascular conditions.

A lot of food-sourced supplements not only guard against disease and breakdown of health, but they also improve the metabolic system and healthy weight maintenance. It makes sense that keeping your body balanced and healthy would work across the board in maintaining healthy weight as well. As you continue on your Skinny Life journey, I suggest that taking a good EFA supplement is a really good idea.[14]

### Probiotics and a Skinny, Healthy Gut

In the world of natural health professionals of which I've been an interactive part for a very long time, you'll often hear a doctor say, "Most of your health and immune system begins in your gut." These doctors are referring to the multifold benefits of keeping your intestines balanced. This includes eating a low-sugar, low-starch diet so that unhealthy gut bacteria don't form and populate, and also eating or supplementing with foods that balance the gut with beneficial bacteria, or probiotics. Many health benefits occur from having large, healthy populations of beneficial or "friendly" flora in our intestinal tract.

Scientists have known for some time that probiotics are necessary for many of the body's processes, ranging from cancer prevention to immune function. Unfortunately, poor diets and lifestyle choices destroy our bodies' beneficial bacteria, decreasing the body's immune function and leaving the body open to harmful microorganisms, such as salmonella and E. coli. Research shows that ingesting probiotics through foods or supplementation causes improvements in things like digestive disorders and enhanced immune function.

Those benefits *alone* are reason enough to eat plenty of the fermented foods that we discussed in chapter 9, or to supplement with a high-quality, multiple-strain probiotic formula. But the added benefit of a healthy gut is also a skinnier gut, according to a research study reported by the European Journal of Clinical Nutrition.[15]

In a study conducted by scientists in Japan, intake of probiotics showed significant reductions in abdominal visceral and subcutaneous fat areas, as well as body weight, BMI, waist and hip circumferences, and body fat mass. Researchers felt that the reduction in visceral fat was singularly important because an excess accumulation of visceral fat is primarily involved in metabolic disorders.[16]

Other studies suggest that imbalance in the intestinal bacteria could result in obesity, systemic inflammation, and metabolic dysfunction. The use of probiotics to balance the gut against obesity and myriad other ailments could be another great tool in your Skinny Life Toolbox.

### Fiber

You've probably sat through a TV commercial or two on the benefits of fiber for constipation. But the story about fiber is way more exciting for Skinny Lifers! Researchers at the *Journal of the American Medical Association* studied the effects of dietary fiber on weight gain and cardiovascular disease in young adults. They found that high-fiber diets may protect against obesity and cardiovascular disease by lowering insulin levels. The current recommendation of fiber intake by the American Heart Association is 20 to 30 grams per day, which they believe will help curtail rising obesity rates in the US.[17]

Most Americans get half that amount. Plant-based fiber also acts as a "prebiotic" for the probiotic flora to colonize in your gut. These prebiotic fibers create an environment for probiotic flora to flourish and thereby increase the number and activity of the valuable probiotics in your gut. Acacia fiber, raw wheat bran, and Jerusalem artichoke are some good sources that can be found in a prebiotic supplement. My husband and I use an Acacia fiber supplement every day in addition to eating a high fiber diet. Although it's not the prettiest topic to discuss, we find that with the amount of traveling we do, it is great at preventing constipation in addition to all of the other terrific health benefits!

### Protein for Skinny-On-the-Go

In chapter 9 we discussed the benefits of adequate protein consumption for creating your most beautiful, lean-burning-machine body. But many people find it difficult to get the amount of protein we need every day to achieve our fit best. One of the best ways to meet our protein requirements is to use a high-quality protein powder once a day for a snack or a meal replacement. Either a high-quality whey protein or a rice protein for vegans is fine. Make sure you're not choosing one that is for super body builders because you could end up with a lot of ingredients you don't want or need. I love mixing my protein with berries or other low-sugar fruits, or even a banana and a little peanut butter for a day when my activities require extra carbs to burn, like after a long bike ride or hike. It is delicious, filling, and keeps me satisfied and energized for hours! Your favorite protein powder will become a great Skinny Life super-tool to pull out every single day.

> There is only one major disease and that is malnutrition. All ailments and afflictions to which we may fall heir are directly traceable to this major disease.
> —D. W. Cavanaugh, MD, Cornell University

The living complexes and key nutrition in high-quality supplements contribute to and improve thousands of critical metabolic functions in your body like cell repair, collagen manufacture, circulation and many others. Supplements containing proteins, vitamins, minerals, and enzymes, along with cofactors, help keep these complex functions actively working in your body. If any of these are missing, the body will rob its own stores to make up the difference, depleting itself in other areas.

Remember, our goal at Skinny Life is to arm you with all of the tools and information you need to gain every advantage toward your greatest health, weight, and future!

## Skinny Life Toolbox

### Supplement Your Journey to Success!

Consider the power of supplements to super boost your success in the Skinny Life journey. I recommend at a minimum that you get a good protein powder and fiber supplement and make sure you're taking a good multivitamin. Do your own research online. Ask at your local health-food store what their best brands or choices would be. Integrate these into your regimen every single day. You'll be giving your body a big advantage, which you'll start to notice very quickly!

# Affirmations

What I put in my body either enhances or
diminishes my health.
I chose to enhance my health in every way I can.

I will make it my business to know what key nutrients
my body needs for optimum health.

The micronutrients in my body can make
a significant difference in my weight and health.

I'm eager and open to learning about foods and
nutritional supplements that can make me
healthier and more fit.

Optimum nutrition will help create optimum
health in my body.

I feel better and feel my body responding positively
to the right nutritional supplements.

I love to arm myself with every weight loss advantage!

# 12

# Skinny Life Summary

Life is a journey of thousands of ups and downs. Along the way you need a handbook that can be a source of truth and inspiration, a source of help that encourages you as a whole person. When I wrote this book I wanted it to be one of those sources for you, one that might help you break through the confusion and frustration of excess weight and the numerous negative effects it can thrust upon your life. It is my hope that you will find comfort, direction, and support again and again in these pages as you navigate your way to good health, fitness, and happiness.

You shouldn't have to waste your precious time on earth bogged down with the belief that being healthy and fit is complicated and unreachable. You can dismiss that lie forever because the Skinny Life lifestyle allows you to live that natural, fit, slim life for all the right reasons, armed with all of the right information. We eat well and eat smart, loving the foods that love us back. We maximize our time spent with our total body power moves and thoroughly enjoy our time being active. We delight in coming up with creative ways to enjoy moving our bodies through life, sharing that time with people we love, and feeling the joy of it in our spirits!

## Set a New Standard

It's difficult to do something different in your life if you are uninformed, unprepared, or uninvolved in your own health. Hopefully through this Skinny Life reading journey you feel more involved, informed, and prepared to live a much better life for yourself. Within each breath of this journey you have choices and opportunities. Only one person can set the standard for how you will live your life and take care of yourself: you. You need to do all you can in a balanced way to stay healthy and well.

**Skinny Life Bottom Line:** Only one person can set the standard for how you will live your life and take care of yourself: you.

## Consider the Future

Any weight issue you face is usually not an issue that will stop with you. Future generations are being affected, and it's time for all of us to jump in with both feet to help, starting with ourselves first. The Skinny Life journey is holistic and comprehensive and designed to be shared with the people you love and care about: your spouse, children, friends, or coworkers who are close to you. It is often more meaningful to make positive changes together than trying to go solo. If your spouse is resistant, then grab your sister, best friend, or your daughter or son to figure out the most fun ways to integrate the Skinny Life lifestyle.

You know now that your old, dysfunctional eating patterns could have emerged from a lack of connection to yourself, your needs, and the relationship or role that food plays in your life. The new, Skinny Life patterns you are establishing come from a place of love, honor, and respect for yourself, as well as a deep connection to yourself, your needs, and your relationship with food. Many people have discovered that as they live and eat the Skinny Life way, instead of feeling restricted or confined, they feel a brand-new sense of freedom. That's because when a compulsion toward food or eating controls you, as it might have in the past, it also controls your weight, health, confidence, and self-esteem. This leaves you feeling out of control. Now, with the guidance and structure the Skinny Life gives you, your inner beliefs, the new values you have about your health and fitness, and your commitment and self-respect will continue to guide your choices and habits. As they do, you will feel that sense of freedom growing ever stronger.

 **Skinny Life Bottom Line:** The new, Skinny Life patterns you are establishing come from a place of love, honor, and respect for yourself.

In the Skinny Life program we retrain your brain to live and eat the Skinny Life way as if that's the only way you would ever want to do it again. You naturally become a pro at avoiding foods that minimize your health and embracing the foods that maximize your health. Over time, as Skinny Lifers repeat the reminders and affirmations, they transition into honoring their bodies and enjoying that mastery. Many of them used to feel as though it was a burden to make a healthy meal for dinner—now they enjoy doing that! They like being creative in combining all of the tasty, healthy options. They enjoy making their nutritious and delicious eating a priority and the feeling they get from feeding themselves with the best-quality foods. I'm always amazed and thrilled to see how, as they honor and respect their bodies in this way, the positive changes spill over into other areas of their lives and they become more self-honoring in their relationships and careers as well.

## Skinny Life Tips and Tricks

As you move forward now with these important life changes, it's helpful to be able to reduce them as much as possible into bite-size chunks that are easy to remember and can easily be turned into life-time habits. Let's review some of the Skinny Life tips and tricks you can implement in your journey as the new you! Post these on your fridge or computer, or in your smartphone or tablet notes, as simple reminders to live as the new you. Consider them your Skinny Life go-to staples of living fit!

### *Be a Breakfast Champion*

When you get up in the morning, your metabolism has been off duty for many hours. Make sure you eat something within the first hour of waking to kick your metabolism back into gear. A banana with a little nut butter or a bowl of berries with a small handful of walnuts or almonds is a great choice! Live enzymes in the fruit help digestion get moving and the nuts support steady burning release of energy. The National Weight Control Registry says people who have lost more than thirty pounds and have kept it off are people who eat breakfast.[1]

### Eat Small, Steady Meals

Eat something every three to four hours to prevent excessive hunger and stabilize your blood sugar. It's never good to ignore real hunger because it causes your body to increase fat-storing enzymes. Be able to respond to your hunger quickly by carrying whole veggies, fruits, and nuts wherever you go.

### Choose Satisfied, Not Stuffed

Most people are conditioned to eat what's on their plate. As you eat your meal, keep checking your fullness. On a scale of 1 to 10, with 10 being completely full, stop at 7. This will increase your awareness of how satisfied you are at a meal. You should never, ever feel an uncomfortably full sensation at the end of a meal. That means you have eaten too much and are overfull!

### Drink Water

Drink ten to twelve cups (80 to 96 ounces) of water each day to stay hydrated and to help flush toxins. Try keeping a bottle of water next to you all day. This makes it easier to track how much water you've had to drink. Thirst is often mistaken for hunger. When you feel hungry, hydrate first and then check for real hunger.

### *Eat for Body, Not Emotions*

Recognize when you are feeling stressed or emotionally distraught, and immediately plan non-eating strategies to soothe yourself. Go for a walk out in beautiful nature, attend a worship meeting, go to the mall to walk and be around people, call a friend, take a bath, or watch a funny movie. Look for ways to feel more connected to yourself and your community.

### *Hunger Is Never an Emergency*

People run to food from a primitive urge of fearing starvation. You are not going to starve, so relax. When you first feel hunger sensations, realize that's normal and nothing to fear. It's your body doing what it's supposed to do in its metabolic process. Before you dive in to a big meal or eat something you will regret later, try these steps:

1. Drink a big glass of water to make sure it's not thirst.
2. Eat a piece of fresh fruit or some crunchy veggies with a small handful of nuts to see if you just needed a snack.
3. If you're still hungry and need a larger meal, choose one that includes lots of leafy greens and a low-fat protein source.

### *Know Your Go-To Foods*

If you commit to eating at least one large salad every day plus one fresh fruit smoothie, you will get a big chunk of your necessary SAINT foods. Making this a hard-and-fast habit will create more healing and overall satisfaction in your everyday eating and allow you to get the daily requirement of nine servings of delicious fruits and veggies no matter what!

### *Stay in Your Move Groove*

Staying on your feet an extra two-and-a-half hours per day can help burn off thirty-three pounds per year, according to a Mayo Clinic study.[2] See yourself as a mover and shaker every day!

### *Laugh Your Way Skinny*

Laughter is a form of exercise. It lowers blood pressure and heart rate and improves lung capacity, just to name a few benefits. One study showed that laughing one hundred to two hundred times a day is the equivalent of rowing for ten minutes![3] Laugh big and laugh often.

### *Good Night, Sleep Tight*

Slim people sleep two more hours per week than overweight people, says a study from Eastern Virginia Medical School. Keeping up with your sleep increases the appetite-suppressing hormones, leptin and ghrelin.[4] Go to bed twenty minutes earlier each night, and you will help your body accomplish your goal!

### *Visualize the New You*

Every night as you're drifting off to sleep, visualize yourself at your ideal weight. Picture the way you'll look and the things you'll be doing as the new fit, slim you. Remember, your mind is the most powerful weight-loss tool you have.

 **Skinny Life Bottom Line:** Your mind is the most powerful weight-loss tool you have.

By implementing these simple lifestyle choices, you will begin to lose weight, trim down, and firm up naturally.

## The Power of Choice

Owning our power to choose allows us to surrender old thoughts, self-beliefs, and habits that have kept us from being all that we could be. When we deliberately choose to release all of those obstacles and replace them with the things we know will bring success into our lives, choice by choice we reaffirm the tremendous power God has given us. We are not victims of poor health or excessive weight. We are created with the free will to choose. Each choice shapes and defines what we will have or not have, what we will be or not be. Our choices thus far have shaped the lives we are living.

 **Skinny Life Bottom Line:** Our choices thus far have shaped the lives we are living.

By making choices from this new place of information, awareness, and connection, we will become renewed in our bodies and minds, never again enslaved to misery. As you move forward in the Skinny Life journey and make these new, positive, life-giving choices, you will begin to reshape your body and your life. If you keep choosing the same old thoughts, beliefs, and habits, then your body, health, and life will stay the same. Your choice is right here, right now in this moment . . . and the next . . . and the next . . . and the next . . .

Will you claim the power this very moment holds for you and choose deliberately to do the next thing that moves you forward down your lifetime path of success? Become observant of every moment to think, speak, and take action with deliberate awareness that you are creating something new and amazing.

Be ready to make new choices each day and don't ever let old choices get in the way of your new masterpiece: you!

When you achieve this natural level of self-mastery in the Skinny Life, it becomes very exciting. You feel better at a core level when you are living in excellence and control. In contrast to other diets and programs you may have tried in the past, where you felt it was about pain, punishment, or deprivation, with Skinny Life you should feel as if you are giving yourself more than you ever have—that you are truly understanding what your body and mind need and how to live out that truth for the rest of your life.

> You will develop a natural mastery over your eating and a comfortable, easy relationship with food.

As you continually reinforce your new habits by surrounding yourself with support, encouragement, and tools, you will develop a mastery over your eating and a comfortable, easy relationship with food. You will also develop a more natural love for movement and an automatic system to integrate it into your life each day. As you learn, follow, and perfect these principles, you will be excited and motivated to do the best things for yourself and your body, because you deserve the best.

# Skinny Life Toolbox

## Count Your Successes

It's important to acknowledge yourself as you move through this wonderful Skinny Life journey of self-renewal. Every time you make a good eating choice, weave in healthy movement, or even just catch yourself thinking like a truly healthy person, take the time to acknowledge yourself in some way. I recommend setting aside a page in your smartphone notebook or in a real one, titling it something like: "I'm Succeeding in My Skinny Life Journey!" or "I'm Doing It!" With each little success, no matter how small, give yourself a little star or symbol that says you're one step closer to total Skinny Life mastery!

> The fact is, you have the ability to change anything in your life!

You can go forward in your Skinny Life journey knowing that you are have everything you need. You have enough strength, resolve, and determination. The fact is, you have the ability to change anything in your life!

Now that you've had an opportunity to read this book and to begin to connect to yourself and your body in a deeper and more meaningful way, decide now that you will never again disconnect from your own body, its value, and the precious temple it provides for you to express all God created you to express here on this earth.

Life is too short to live in a body that you don't or can't enjoy.

If you stay connected and follow the simple strategies laid out in this book, you will begin to lose weight easily and permanently, and more importantly, you will become masterful in your health and fitness forever! *Skinny Life* will continue to be your guide to experiencing permanent weight mastery without ever dieting again.

# Acknowledgments

In writing this book I feel that it's important to acknowledge the people throughout the years who have all woven pieces of their threads into this blanket of work that I love sharing.

First of all, to my clients who have been open and receptive to the truths that I share and have trusted me to guide them through important pieces of their lives. That is an honor I never take for granted and it is what gives me the greatest joy. Thanks for teaching me through your vulnerability as much as I teach you. Thanks to the countless mentors, teachers, guides, and coaches I've learned from, studied with, and shared thoughts and ideas with. You are too numerous to name, but you know who you are and I love you and appreciate you immeasurably.

Thanks to my precious agent, Ted Squires, and Byron Williamson for receiving my ideas with open hearts and for deciding they needed to be shared with as many people as possible.

Thanks for Josh and Karen—you two are like earth angels who see the bigger vision and selflessly work to make sure it is supported in every way you can. None of this Skinny Life journey could go forward without the teamwork you guys bring to the table every day. Thanks for hanging in there through the highs and lows. I love you both.

Big thanks to the whole Worthy support team: Jeanna, Sherrie, Dennis, and Leeanna. And to my terrific editing duo, Holly and Jennifer. Working with the two of you has been a total pleasure and you've helped make this a better book.

Total gratitude to my best friend Janet Davis, who always encourages and supports my ideas and ventures with total support and love, and helps me get down life's bumpy roads. You are my sister forever.

Thank you, Mom, for being a true pioneer in health and wellness starting from the time I was in your womb. This all started with your commitment to the truth about health and your dedication to giving your nine children the greatest health advantage possible. You made it look easy because you loved health, truth, and us so much. You are amazing!

Heartfelt, unstoppable love for my beautiful, precious kids— Preston, Shannon, and Kelly—who tell me they're proud of my work and me. Each one of you in your perfect uniqueness is a whole universe of joy to me.

I give loving thanks and undying gratitude the most amazing, loving man in the world, my husband, Mark Victor Hansen. Thank you for pushing me out in front in those moments when I would rather retreat to the back and not get noticed. Thanks for insisting I'm brilliant even when I'm feeling lackluster. You make life a happier place to live.

Thank you to God for everything and for giving me so much to love.

# Appendix A
## THIEF Foods—Foods to Avoid

As we learned in chapter 9, the problem with THIEF foods is that *they highjack important endocrine functions.* They steal your health. The following foods provide little to no nourishment and often create more havoc than good. Avoid these foods.

### Soda

One can of soda contains ten teaspoons of sugar, and diet versions with aspartame or artificial sweeteners are not proven to be safe for the body. Use sparkling mineral water or flavored, unsweetened sparkling water with a touch of Stevia leaf sweetener. Try the flavored Stevia for a special treat!

### Bakery Goods (especially processed packaged ones)
- Muffins
- Doughnuts or Danish pastries
- Dessert cakes or Cupcakes
- Croissants

### White Bread

Low nutritional value. High glycemic (blood sugar) load. Avoid any form of white bread. Use 100 percent whole-wheat versions of all breads, wraps, or tortillas, preferably sprouted or non-GMO if possible.

### White Rice

No nutritional value. High glycemic load. Choose brown rice with three times the fiber and more B vitamins.

## Bagels

Avoid these, especially the white ones. Choose 100 percent whole-wheat non-GMO or sprouted organic toast with a tablespoon of low-fat cream cheese or nut butter.

## Sugary Cereals

Skip these. Choose 100 percent whole-grain cereals with less than six grams of sugar, at least five grams of fiber or more, and five to six grams of protein or more.

## Stick Margarine

Margarine contains bad trans fats. Choose a teaspoon or less of real, natural butter. They make spreadable versions now that are easy to use.

## Jarred Tomato Sauce or Barbecue Sauce with Sugar

Some sauces contain whopping amounts of sugar. Hidden sources of sugar create fat bellies. Either make your own or look for sugar-free versions. Do a web search before you shop so you know which ones are which. The sugar-free sauces actually taste better and fresher!

## Bacon

High fat, super-high sodium, low protein. Three slices contain 435 milligrams of sodium, about one-fifth of the average adult's daily allowance. Use low-fat turkey bacon or Canadian bacon instead. It's tasty and high in protein.

**Processed Meats**

- Hot Dogs
- Bologna
- Sausages (unless they're low-fat chicken or turkey)
- Salami or any lunchmeat made of little bits of meat parts put together.

Opt for whole cut deli meats with minimal processing and lower salt and preservative. There are plenty of them!

**Deep Fried Foods**

When food is fried, the nutritional value is cooked out and high temperatures can form toxic chemical compounds in the food. Grilling, baking, boiling, poaching, simmering, or using a wok are all far better options.

**Canned Soups with Monosodium Glutamate (MSG)**

Monosodium Glutamate (MSG) is superconcentrated salt that can trip up weight-loss efforts. If you eat canned soup, choose organic or ones with no MSG.

**High Fructose Corn Syrup (HFCS)**

Avoid all salad dressings, cereals, or any food containing HFCS. Olive oil or canola oil with balsamic vinegar or fresh lemon and sea salt is the best way to go.

# Appendix B
## SAINT Foods—Foods to Eat

We learned in chapter 9 that SAINT foods are *satisfying, active, ideal, natural,* and *therapeutic.* The following foods provide high levels of energy and nutrition without being easily converted to body fat. Stock your pantry with these.

**Veggies**
- green leafy lettuce
- kale
- cabbage
- spinach
- turnip greens
- Swiss chard
- broccoli
- cauliflower
- bok choy
- green beans
- asparagus
- celery
- red, green, yellow peppers
- zucchini
- eggplant
- nopal cactus leaves
- turnips
- rutabagas
- carrots
- beets—all colors
- sweet potatoes
- squash
- pumpkin
- avocados
- tomatoes
- cucumbers
- jalapeños
- onions

**Fruits**
- apples—green and red
- kiwi
- strawberries
- blueberries
- blackberries
- cantaloupe
- watermelon
- honeydew
- pomegranate
- peaches
- nectarines
- apricots
- papaya
- oranges
- grapefruits
- lemons

**Herbs**
- cilantro
- parsley
- rosemary
- oregano
- garlic

**Beans**
- lentils
- black beans
- red beans
- garbanzo beans
- pinto beans
- white beans
- lima beans
- fat-free bean dip
- peas

**Lunch Meats**
- turkey cold cuts
- canned: tuna, chicken breast, salmon

**Proteins**
- chicken breast
- turkey breast
- lean cuts of beef
- buffalo or bison meat
- salmon
- trout
- white fish (cod, halibut, etc.)
- tofu
- miso

**Other Proteins**
- low-fat cottage cheese
- low-fat Greek yogurt (plain)
- low-fat kefir cheese
- parmesan cheese
- 2% low-fat cheddar cheese
- skim, soy, or almond milk

**Whole Grains**
- quinoa
- brown rice
- brown-rice pasta
- steel-cut oats
- 100 percent sprouted-grain bread

**Nuts and Nut Butters**
*(eat 1 oz or 2 tbsp 5 days per week)*
- almond butter
- peanut butter
- cashew butter
- almonds
- walnuts
- cashews
- sunflower seeds
- pumpkin seeds
- Brazil nuts *(2 per day)*

**Teas**
- green tea
- herb tea
- black tea
- flavored tea

**Condiments and Oils**
- agave
- stevia
- salsas
- olive oil
- coconut oil
- grape-seed oil
- sesame oil

**Spices**
- low-sodium soy sauce
- balsamic vinegar
- sea salt (with brown minerals visible)
- garlic powder
- cinnamon
- flavorful spice mixes

# Notes

## Chapter 1: It's about a Relationship

1. "The U.S. Weight Loss Market: 2015 Status Report and Forecast," Marketdata Enterprises Inc., January 2015, https://www.bharatbook.com/healthcare-market-research-reports-467678/the-us-weight-loss-market-2014-status-report-forecast.html.
2. Traci Mann et al., "Medicare's Search for Effective Obesity Treatments: Diets Are Not the Answer," *American Psychologist* 62, no. 3 (April 2007): 220–33, http://psycnet.apa.org/?&fa=main. doiLanding&doi=10.1037/0003-066X.62.3.220.
3. "Obesity Information," American Heart Association, updated February 27, 2014, http://www.heart.org/HEARTORG/GettingHealthy/WeightManagement/Obesity/Obesity-Information_UCM_307908_Article.jsp.
4. "What Is Childhood Obesity?," American Heart Association, updated August 4, 2014, http://www.heart.org/HEARTORG/GettingHealthy/HealthierKids/ChildhoodObesity/What-is-childhood-obesity_UCM_304347_Article.jsp.
5. "Overweight in Children," American Heart Association, updated August 4, 2014, http://www.heart.org/HEARTORG/GettingHealthy/HealthierKids/ChildhoodObesity/Overweight-in-Children_UCM_304054_Article.jsp.
6. Ibid.
7. David Schlundt, PhD, "General Information about Weight Cycling," Health Psychology, Vanderbilt University Department of Psychology, http://www.vanderbilt.edu/AnS/psychology/health_psychology/ScientificStudy.htm.
8. Ibid.

## Chapter 2: The Amazing Body God Has Given You

1. J. Michael Gonzalez-Campoy, "Obesity and Health Consequences," EndocrineWeb, Endocrine Disorders, March 25, 2015, http://www.endocrineweb.com/conditions/obesity/obesity-health-consequences.
2. Earl Nightingale, *Lead the Field* audio series (Wheeling, IL: Nightingale-Conant, 2012), www.nightingaleconant.com.

## Chapter 3: Stop Weighing and Worrying

1. Michael Boschmann et al., "Water-Induced Thermogenesis," *Journal of Clinical Endocrinology and Metabolism* 88, no. 12 (December 2003): 6015–19, published online July 2, 2013, http://dx.doi.org/10.1210/jc.2003-030780.
2. Yu Xu et al., "Prevalence and Control of Diabetes in Chinese Adults," *Journal of the American Medical Association* 310, no. 9 (September 4, 2013): 948–59, doi:10.1001/jama.2013.168118.

3. Ibid.
4. Ibid.
5. Daryl Loo, "China 'Catastrophe' Hits 114 Million as Diabetes Spreads," *Bloomberg Business*, September 3, 2013, http://www.bloomberg.com/news/articles/2013-09-03/china-catastrophe-hits-114-million-as-diabetes-spreads.

**Chapter 4: Weight and Health Issues Start in Your Mind**
1. J. Bruce Moseley et al., "A Controlled Trial of Arthroscopic Surgery for Osteoarthritis of the Knee," *New England Journal of Medicine* 347, no. 2 (July 11, 2002): 81–88, doi: 10.1056/NEJMoa013259.
2. Eric Manheimer et al., "Acupuncture for Treatment of Irritable Bowel Syndrome," Cochrane Library, May 16, 2012, http://onlinelibrary.wiley.com/doi/10.1002/14651858.CD005111.pub3/abstract;jsessionid=34609 1B48E7F3CDBD5D3F3C1179D877D.f03t03. See also Ted J. Kaptchuk et al., "Placebos without Deception: A Randomized Controlled Trial in Irritable Bowel Syndrome," *PLOS One*, December 22, 2010, http://www.plosone.org/article/info%3Adoi%2F10.1371%2Fjournal.pone.0015591.
3. Daniel J. DeNoon, "Asthma Study Shows Placebo Can Help Symptoms," WebMD Health News, July 13, 2011, drug.http://www.webmd.com/asthma/news/20110713/asthma-study-shows-placebo-can-help-symptoms.
4. Irving Kirsch, "Challenging Received Wisdom: Antidepressants and the Placebo Effect," *McGill Journal of Medicine* 11, no. 2 (November 2008): 219–22, http://www.ncbi.nlm.nih.gov/pmc/articles/PMC2582668/.

**Chapter 8: The New Me: My Mind**
1. Dr. Candace Pert, *Molecules of Emotion: The Science behind Mind-Body Medicine* (New York: Simon & Schuster, 1999).

**Chapter 9: The New Me: My Eating**
1. "Obesity and Overweight," World Health Organization fact sheet, updated January 2015, http://www.who.int/mediacentre/factsheets/fs311/en/.
2. The Biotechnology Institute, "The Gene Revolution in Food," *Your World: Biotechnology and You* 10, no. 1 (2000), http://biomed.brown.edu/arise/resources/docs/yw10_1.pdf; "GMO Dangers," Institute for Responsible Technology, accessed April 28, 2015, http://www.responsibletechnology.org/gmo-dangers.
3. K. H. Pietiläinen et al., "Does Dieting Make You Fat? A Twin Study," *International Journal of Obesity* 36 (March 2012): 456–64, http://www.nature.com/ijo/journal/v36/n3/full/ijo2011160a.html.
4. Alison E. Field et al., "Relation between Dieting and Weight Change among Preadolescents and Adolescents," *Pediatrics* 112, no. 4 (October 1, 2003): 900–906, http://pediatrics.aappublications.org/content/112/4/900.

5.  Jess Haines and Dianne Neumark-Sztainer, "Prevention of Obesity and Eating Disorders: A Consideration of Shared Risk Factors," *Health Education Research* 21, no. 6 (September 8, 2006): 770–82, http://her.oxfordjournals.org/content/21/6/770.

6.  Thomas L. Halton and Frank B. Hu, "The Effects of High Protein Diets on Thermogenesis, Satiety and Weight Loss: A Critical Review," *Journal of the American College of Nutrition* 23, no. 5 (2004) 373–85, http://www.tandfonline.com/doi/abs/10.1080/07315724.2004.10719381#.VR6fBbpN3zI.

7.  B. J. Rolls, J. A. Ello-Martin, and B. C. Tohill, "What Can Intervention Studies Tell Us about the Relationship between Fruit and Vegetable Consumption and Weight Management?," *Nutrition Reviews* 62, no. 1 (January 2004): 1–17.

8.  Wayne C. Miller et al., "Dietary Fat, Sugar, and Fiber Predict Body Fat Content," *Journal of the Academy of Nutrition and Dietetics* 94, no. 6, (June 1994): 612–15, http://www.andjrnl.org/article/0002-8223(94)90155-4/abstract.

9.  K. A. McAuley et al., "Comparison of High-Fat and High-Protein Diets with a High-Carbohydrate Diet in Insulin-Resistant Obese Women," *Diabetologia* 48, no. 1 (January 2005): 8–16, http://www.ncbi.nlm.nih.gov/pubmed/15616799.

10. Halton and Hu, "Effects of High Protein Diets; L. J. Appel et al., "Effects of Protein, Monounsaturated Fat, and Carbohydrate Intake on Blood Pressure and Serum Lipids: Results of the OmniHeart Randomized Trial," *Journal of the American Medical Association* 294, no. 19 (November 16, 2005):2455–64, http://www.ncbi.nlm.nih.gov/pubmed/16287956.

11. *Dictionary.com*, s.v. "food," http://dictionary.reference.com/browse/food?s=t.

12. Connecticut College, "Are Oreos Addictive? Research Says Yes." ScienceDaily, October 15, 2013, www.sciencedaily.com/releases/2013/10/131015123341.htm.

13. Byron J. Richards, "Insulin, Leptin, and Blood Sugar—Why Diabetic Medication Fails," Wellness Resources, August 20, 2012, www.wellnessresources.com/tips/articles/insulin_leptin_and_blood_sugar_why_diabetic_medication_fails/.

14. Charles Q. Choi, "Does Intermittent Fasting Have Benefits? Science Suggests Yes," LiveScience, November 25, 2014, http://www.livescience.com/48888-intermittent-fasting-benefits-weight-loss.html.

15. S. Lenzen, "The Mechanisms of Alloxan- and Streptozotocin-Induced Diabetes," *Diabetologia* 51, no. 2 (February 2008): 216–26, http://www.ncbi.nlm.nih.gov/pubmed/18087688.

16. Ibid. See also A. Mrozikiewicz et al., "Blood Levels of Alloxan in Children with Insulin-Dependent Diabetes Mellitus," *Acta Diabetol* 31, no. 4 (December 1994): 236–7, http://www.ncbi.nlm.nih.gov/pubmed/7888696;

K. Hamden et al., "1α,25 Dihydroxyvitamin D3: Therapeutic and Preventive Effects against Oxidative Stress, Hepatic, Pancreatic and Renal Injury in Alloxan-Induced Diabetes in Rats," *Journal of Nutritional Science and Vitaminology* 55, no. 3 (July 15, 2009): 215-22, https://www. jstage.jst.go.jp/article/jnsv/55/3/55_3_215/_article; T. Szkudelski, "The Mechanism of Alloxan and Streptozotocin Action in B Cells of the Rat Pancreas," *Physiological Research* 50, no. 6 (2001): 537–46, http://www.ncbi. nlm.nih.gov/pubmed/11829314.

17. Luc Tappy, Kim-Anne Lê, "Metabolic Effects of Fructose and the Worldwide Increase in Obesity," *Physiological Reviews* 90, no. 1 (January 2010): 23–46, doi: 10.1152/physrev.00019.2009.

18. Ibid.

19. Yuren Wei et al., "Fructose-Induced Stress Signaling in the Liver Involves Methylglyoxal," *Nutrition & Metabolism* 10 (2013): 32, http://www. nutritionandmetabolism.com/content/10/1/32.

20. Suzanne Devkota and Donald K. Layman, "Increased Ratio of Dietary Carbohydrate to Protein Shifts the Focus of Metabolic Signaling from Skeletal Muscle to Adipose," *Nutrition and Metabolism* (London) 8 (March 4, 2011): 13, doi: 10.1186/1743-7075-8-13.

21. "Aging Changes in Body Shape," *Medline Plus Medical Encyclopedia*, updated November 16, 2012, http://www.nlm.nih.gov/medlineplus/ency/ article/003998.htm; Wayne Campbell, "Elderly Women May Benefit from Higher Amounts of Protein," Purdue University News, March 24, 2014, http://www.purdue.edu/newsroom/releases/2014/Q1/elderly-women-may-benefit-from-higher-amounts-of-protein.html; "Protein," The Nutrition Source, Harvard School of Public Health, accessed April 28, 2015, http:// www.hsph.harvard.edu/nutritionsource/what-should-you-eat/protein/.

22. United States Department of Agriculture, "How Much Food from the Protein Foods Group Is Needed?," USDA ChooseMyPlate.gov, accessed April 28, 2015, http://www.choosemyplate.gov/printpages/ MyPlateFoodGroups/ProteinFoods/food-groups.protein-foods-amount.pdf; Mayo Clinic Staff, "Healthy Diet: Do You Follow Dietary Guidelines?," Mayo Clinic Healthy Lifestyle, February 22, 2013, http://www. mayoclinic.org/healthy-living/nutrition-and-healthy-eating/in-depth/ how-to-eat-healthy/art-20046590.

23. M. J. Franz, "Protein: metabolism and effect on blood glucose levels," *Diabetes Educator,* 23, no. 6 (November–December 1997): 64351, doi: 10.1177/014572179702300603.

24. Cara B. Ebbeling et al., "Effects of Dietary Composition on Energy Expenditure during Weight-Loss Maintenance," *Journal of the American Medical Association* 307, no. 24 (June 27, 2012): 2627–34, http://jama. jamanetwork.com/article.aspx?articleid=1199154.

## Chapter 10: The New Me: My Movement

1.  Mayo Clinic Staff, "Exercise: 7 Benefits of Regular Physical Activity," Mayo Clinic Healthy Lifestyle, February 5, 2014, http://www.mayoclinic.org/healthy-lifestyle/fitness/in-depth/exercise/art-20048389.
2.  Neville Owen et al., "Too Much Sitting: The Population Health Science of Sedentary Behavior," *Exercise and Sport Sciences Reviews* 38, no. 3 (July 2010): 105–13, http://www.ncbi.nlm.nih.gov/pmc/articles/PMC3404815/.
3.  Kelli Miller, "Daily Inactivity, Not Just Lack of Exercise, Could Be Making You Sick," WebMD Fitness and Exercise, January 19, 2010, http://www.webmd.com/fitness-exercise/20100119/prolonged-sitting-boosts-bad-health.
4.  D. W. Dunstan et al., "Television Viewing Time and Mortality: The Australian Diabetes, Obesity and Lifestyle Study," *Circulation* 121, no. 3 (January 26, 2010): 384–91, published online January 11, 2010, http://circ.ahajournals.org/content/121/3/384.
5.  Ibid.
6.  Owen et al., "Too much sitting."
7.  Gregory W. Heath, "Made to Move," The American College of Sports Medicine *ACSM Fit Society Page,* Summer 2012, http://www.acsm.org/docs/fit-society-page/acsmfspsummer2012.pdf.
8.  Ibid.
9.  David R. Bassett Jr., Patrick L. Schneider, and Gertrude E. Huntington, "Physical Activity in an Old Order Amish Community." *Medicine and Science in Sports and Exercise* 36, no. 1 (January 2004): 79–85, http://citeseerx.ist.psu.edu/viewdoc/download?doi=10.1.1.327.1998&rep=rep1&type=pdf.
10. Ibid.
11. Ibid.
12. "The Amish Obesity Studies," World Life Expectancy, accessed April 29, 2015, http://www.worldlifeexpectancy.com/the-amish-obesity-studies.
13. Ibid.
14. Jeannine Stein, "Strength Training Does More Than Bulk Up Muscles," *Los Angeles Times,* February 13, 2011, http://articles.latimes.com/2011/feb/13/health/la-he-adv-strength-training-20110213.
15. "Why Strength Training?," Centers for Disease Control and Prevention Physical Activity, last reviewed February 24, 2011, http://www.cdc.gov/physicalactivity/growingstronger/why/index.html.
16. Allison Van Dusen, "Best Ways to Build Muscle at Any Age," *Forbes,* August 13, 2007, http://www.forbes.com/2007/08/10/health-fitness-muscle-forbeslife-cx_avd_0813health.html.
17. Rebecca A. Seguin et al., *Growing Stronger: Strength Training for Older Adults* (Boston: Tufts University, 2002), 8, http://www.cdc.gov/nccdphp/dnpa/physical/growing_stronger/growing_stronger.pdf.
18. "Why Strength Training?," Centers for Disease Control.

19. Cornell Food & Brand Lab, "Think Fun When Exercising and You'll Eat Less Later," ScienceDaily, July 9, 2014. www.sciencedaily.com/releases/2014/07/140709095929.htm.

20. Ibid.

21. Denise Mann, "Get Sexual for Ultimate Weight Loss," WebMD, reviewed July 1, 2006, http://www.webmd.com/sex-relationships/features/sex-for-weight-loss.

22. Steve Vernon, "Church, Chocolate, Sex and 3 Other Keys to Living Longer," CBS MoneyWatch, April 22, 2011, http://www.cbsnews.com/news/church-chocolate-sex-and-3-other-keys-to-living-longer/.

**Chapter 11: Supplements: God's Miracles in Nature**

1. Rowdy Scheer and Doug Moss, "Dirt Poor: Have Fruits and Vegetables become Less Nutritious?" Earthtalk, *Scientific American*, April 27, 2011, http://www.scientificamerican.com/article/soil-depletion-and-nutrition-loss/.

2. John B. Marler and Jeanne R. Wallin, "Human Health, the Nutritional Quality of Harvested Food and Sustainable Farming Systems," Nutrition Security Institute, 2006, http://www.nutritionsecurity.org/pdf/nsi_white%20paper_web.pdf.

3. Jorge Fernandez-Cornejo, Seth Wechsler, Mike Livingston, and Lorraine Mitchell, "Genetically Engineered Crops in the United States," err-162 U.S. Department of Agriculture, Economic Research Service, February 2014, http://www.ers.usda.gov/media/1282246/err162.pdf.

4. Mira Calton, "Modern Mediocrity: The Truth about our Food Supply," *Be More!*, Accessed April 29, 2015, http://be.well.org/modern-mediocrity-truth-food-supply/.

5. Donald Davis, quoted in Scheer and Moss, "Dirt Poor."

6. Calton, "Modern Mediocrity."

7. ibid.

8. Brian Halweil, "Still No Free Lunch: Nutrient Levels in US Food Supply Eroded by Pursuit of High Yields," The Organic Center, September 2007, https://www.organic-center.org/reportfiles/YieldsReport.pdf.

9. Caroline Praderio, "Is Vitamin Deficiency Making You Fat?" *Prevention*, February 3, 2015, https://au.lifestyle.yahoo.com/prevention/a/26183620/is-vitamin-deficiency-making-you-fat.

10. Ivonne Sluijs et al., "Dietary Carotenoid Intake is Associated with Lower Prevalence of Metabolic Syndrome in Middle-Aged and Elderly Men," *Journal of Nutrition* 139, no. 5 (May 2009): 987–92, http://jn.nutrition.org/content/139/5/987.

11. Y. J. Foss, "Vitamin D Deficiency Is the Cause of Common Obesity," *Medical Hypotheses* 72, no. 3 (March 2009): 314–21, http://www.medical-hypotheses.com/article/S0306-9877(08)00528-8/abstract.

12. United States Department of Agriculture, "Vegetables," http://www.choosemyplate.gov/food-groups/vegetables.html.

13. Eric Metcalf, "Phytonutrients," WebMD, reviewed October 29, 2014, http://www.webmd.com/diet/phytonutrients-faq.

14. Antonio Paoli et al., "Effects of *n*-3 Polyunsaturated Fatty Acids (ω-3) Supplementation on Some Cardiovascular Risk Factors with a Ketogenic Mediterranean Diet," *Marine Drugs* 13, no. 2 (February 2015): 996–1009, http://www.ncbi.nlm.nih.gov/pmc/articles/PMC4344614/; Tracy Hampton, "Mechanism behind Omega-3 Fatty Acids' Heart Benefits," *Journal of the American Medical Association* 312, no. 9 (September 3, 2014): 882, doi:10.1001/jama.2014.11282.

15. Y. Kadooka et al., "Regulation of Abdominal Adiposity by Probiotics (*Lactobacillus gasseri* SBT2055) in Adults with Obese Tendencies in a Randomized Controlled Trial," *European Journal of Clinical Nutrition* 64 (2010): 636–43, http://dx.doi.org/10.1038/ejcn.2010.19.

16. G. Escobedo, E. López-Ortiz, and I. Torres-Castro, "Gut Microbiota as a Key Player in Triggering Obesity, Systemic Inflammation and Insulin Resistance," *Revista de Investigación Clínica* 66, no. 5 (September–October 2014): 450–9, http://www.ncbi.nlm.nih.gov/pubmed/25695388; Jing-Hua Wang et al., "Fermented *Rhizoma Atractylodis Macrocephalae* Alleviates High Fat Diet-Induced Obesity in Association with Regulation of Intestinal Permeability and Microbiota in Rats," *Scientific Reports* 5 (2015): 8391, online February 16, 2015, doi: 10.1038/srep08391.

17. David S. Ludwig et al., "Dietary Fiber, Weight Gain, and Cardiovascular Disease Risk Factors in Young Adults," *Journal of the American Medical Association* 282, no. 16 (October 27,1999): 1539–46. http://dx.doi.org/10.1001/jama.282.16.1539; "Whole Grains and Fiber," American Heart Association, http://www.heart.org/HEARTORG/GettingHealthy/NutritionCenter/HealthyEating/Whole-Grains-and-Fiber_UCM_303249_Article.jsp.

**Chapter 12: Skinny Life Summary**

1. "NWCR Facts," National Weight Control Registry, accessed April 29, 2015, http://www.nwcr.ws/research/.

2. Megan McMorris, "8 Secrets of the Naturally Slim," *Prevention*, November 3, 2011, http://www.prevention.com/weight-loss/weight-loss-tips/how-naturally-slim-women-eat.

3. Michael Miller and William F. Fry, "The Effect of Mirthful Laughter on the Human Cardiovascular System," *Medical Hypotheses* 73, no. 5 (November 2009): 636–39, doi: http://dx.doi.org/10.1016/j.mehy.2009.02.044.

4. McMorris, "8 Secrets."

## We Love to Hear from You!

At Skinny Life, we don't ever want you to feel like you have to go it alone. We invite you to write to Crystal or to one of our team members to share your stories and triumphs, ask questions, or just get a shout out or boost of support! Feel free to track your journey and keep us up to date. Take before and after photos and share with our community after you see and feel yourself naturally becoming the best, fit, slim, healthy version of you! Go to http://www.skinnylife.com/category/share/ to share your story to encourage and inspire others!

The **Skinny Life Total Living** online program (www.skinnylife.com) provides daily tips, tricks, and Skinny Boosts to help make your journey easier and more natural and to give you that daily support that can make a big difference.

# About the Author

**Crystal Dwyer Hansen** is an entrepreneur and founder of CrystalVision, Ltd. and Skinny Life. She is a member of the International Coaching Federation and a wellness and nutrition expert. Through Crystal's personal life-change coaching, speaking, CD programs, videos, books, and articles, people all over the world have experienced profound and lasting transformation in relationships, career, health, and wellness. She and her husband, best-selling author and entrepreneur Mark Victor Hansen, live in Newport Beach, California.

**WORTHY®**

P U B L I S H I N G

If you enjoyed this book, will you consider sharing the message with others?

- Mention the book in a Facebook post, Twitter update, Pinterest pin, blog post, or upload a picture through Instagram.

- Recommend this book to those in your small group, book club, workplace, and classes.

- Head over to facebook.com/worthypublishing, "LIKE" the page, and post a comment as to what you enjoyed the most.

- Tweet "I recommend reading #SkinnyLife by @CrystalVision // @worthypub"

- Pick up a copy for someone you know who would be challenged and encouraged by this message.

- Write a book review online.

You can subscribe to Worthy Publishing's newsletter at worthypublishing.com.

**WORTHY PUBLISHING**
**FACEBOOK PAGE**

**WORTHY PUBLISHING**
**WEBSITE**